What people are saying

Hedy Wiebe's journey from devastation to the writing of *There's a Place Deep inside Called Courage* is a must-read for anyone who has ever doubted or experienced God's healing power and grace. It's a book for all who are in the professions of mending broken bones, muddled brains, unintelligible speech, unbearable pain as well as those who provide hope and love to the hurting hearts of family and friends.

The presence of Jesus Christ and the power of the Holy Spirit are peppered throughout the book as a testament that, just as Hedy found that place deep inside called Courage, so can all who place their trust in God.

—Enedelia Olivarez-Arnal, M.Ed., LPC,
Owner of E.E.O. Professional Corporation,
National Board of Certified Counselors (2006-2019)

If you're in need of courage to go on living, if life as you have known it is gone, you will benefit from taking this journey with someone who has been given the words to describe how she survived and came back from being shattered to live more richly than ever before. If you are in that place, it will take courage to read her story. Read it in digestible portions. Know ahead of time that it has an ending that is both believable and beyond anything you might hope for in your own imaginings.

—Dr. William Davis, PhD, C. Psych.
Retired Winnipeg Police Service Psychologist

There's a Place Deep inside Called Courage is a story of incredible spiritual love and courage, personal and intimate. Hedy bravely and humbly brings you with her on her journey of every conceivable emotion and physical struggle, right to victory through the love of Christ. If ever you have doubted the personal, intimate love of God in your life, or have lost faith, this is the story for you. Like me, I trust you will be spiritually healed, emotionally edified, and inspirationally renewed.

—Wendy Kroeker
Professional Artist and Instructor

"We are of good courage, I say, and are willing rather to be absent from the [human] *body, and to be at home* [in heaven] *with the Lord"* (2 Corinthians 5:8, ASV).

These words from Paul pertain to all believers, but they obviously carry particular significance for Hedy. You can't help but be envious of Hedy … not for the devastating experience she faced, but rather for the amazingly intimate relationship she has with Jesus, and how it kept her throughout her lengthy, grueling years of rehabilitation. It has made her the beautiful child of God she is today. "Inspired" and "blessed" are the best words I can think of to describe my feelings after reading Hedy's story.

—Ron Kroeker
Retired Owner and Creative Director at Country Graphics and Printing
Illustrator of *Donnie's Little Red Wagon*

Awesome! A captivating unveiling of a deeply personal and ongoing journey with the Master Healer, set in the aftermath of huge personal loss and tragedy. This work of faith and obedience is tremendously encouraging and inspiring … yet woefully insufficient! After all, as Hedy readily admits, how can you adequately describe a *real*, personal, ongoing encounter with the *living God* in merely human words? With the help of the Holy Spirit, Hedy's work comes as close to this as I have seen in my twenty-plus years of pastoring.

—Darren Plett (BRS)
Community Pastor, Pleasant Valley EMC
(Don and Hedy's home church)

I found Hedy Wiebe's beautiful and inspiring book, *There's a Place Deep inside Called Courage*, both terrifying and captivating at the same time. It's terrifying as Hedy takes you on an unusual journey of unimaginable pain and suffering after a disastrous car accident. But Hedy doesn't leave her readers with only the ashes of a disaster. She captivates and transforms her readers by the way she embraces the loving redemption of a personal and sovereign God who alone can bring beauty out of ashes. Hedy's delightful sense of humour, her tenacious grit and unconquerable faith, as well as her beautiful way of engaging with Jesus, will not only inspire you but transform your perspective on suffering.

—Ron MacLean
Senior Pastor, Gateway Church, Winnipeg, MB
City Pastors Prayer Network
Salt and Light International Team

there's a
PLACE *deep*
inside # CALLED

COURAGE
a memoir

HEDY R. WIEBE
Foreword by August Konkel, Ph.D.

THERE'S A PLACE DEEP INSIDE CALLED COURAGE

Copyright © 2020 by Hedy R. Wiebe

Print ISBN: 978-1-4866-1924-5
eBook ISBN: 978-1-4866-1925-2

Word Alive Press
119 De Baets Street, Winnipeg, MB R2J 3R9
www.wordalivepress.ca

WORD ALIVE
—P R E S S—

Cataloguing in Publication may be obtained through Library and Archives Canada

For my Don, my brave heart.

Acknowledgements

Writing this book was an act of flat out obedience and trust in my heavenly Father. Ill-equipped? Yes. Confused and unwilling? Yes. In pain and weary? Yes. Through the years, the overwhelming desire to finish what He gave me to do prevailed. Love won out because God cradled me in His keeping. His Holy Spirit never let go … not once. You are holding His never-letting-go love in your hands.

Since 1999, God has strategically positioned people in my life.

Grateful thanks go to the police officers of the Town of Selkirk RCMP detachment; first responders; ER staff at Seven Oaks Hospital in Winnipeg, Manitoba; ambulance drivers and attendants; and the ER doctors, nurses, technicians, and specialists at the Health Sciences Centre (HSC) in Winnipeg. Medically speaking, without them I wouldn't be alive today.

Thank you to the parade, even though my memory is blurry, of medical professionals who came through my hospital room: physical and occupational therapists, and vestibular physiotherapists. I also thank the white-coated doctors I call "the head guys, the legs and ankles guys, the gut guys, the dizzy guys, the bone-break guys, and the step-down guys. These were all better known to me as "the gander and all those goslings," because a teaching hospital employs many doctors in residence who constantly follow their instructor.

Reverently, I thank the many who prayed on my behalf, because prayer chains were activated across Canada by Riverwood Community Church. Gratitude rises when I'm told of intense prayer warriors who supported my family by filling up the ER waiting room for days at HSC. Your prayers were crucial.

Hugs go out to every friend and extended family member who offered our family sips from "cups of cold water" when I couldn't drink for myself physically or spiritually. Liz, the homecare worker: I blow you a kiss wherever you are!

I'm smiling at the memories of everyone who came to visit and chat about their day, and to those who sat wordlessly, gently touching me where it didn't hurt. Gratitude goes to each one who selflessly offered tangible evidence of their love and prayers to our family over the many years of recovery. You know who you are. You are not nameless to me. To those who read God's Word when I couldn't lift my Bible … I believe God's blessing is yours!

When the throes of trauma hit, God brought Dr. Ian Mogilevsky into my life to repeatedly help me navigate my way forward to wellness. Dr. Bill Davis, your ability to speak the language of the head as well as the heart brought much healing to Don and my banged-up emotions. I thank you both.

Esther and Florence, you build up in the Word and faith week after week. Donna and my Mary, each of you continue to offer guidance and words of wisdom and knowledge while leading me deeper into pursuit of Jesus, the one who saved me. I extend warm thanks for the steadfast support of the wonderfully diverse group of women in Bible study group as we met in different homes over the years. I especially thank the Rebekah Group and the Farmhouse Ladies, who've cheered me on during this lengthy writing process. They also prayed when pain and weariness made a lot of noise. To the prayer warrior women at ladies' prayer from Gateway South Community, you care above and beyond "self." Bertha, you patiently saw me through your camera lenses. I love you all.

It is a joyful privilege to link arms and do life together with my church family at Pleasant Valley Church, EMC.

For giving me a room with a view of my town, thanks go to Denis and staff at Rosenort Agro.

Ennie, mi casa es tu casa. You gave me a warm place to write as I waited for God to show me how to put pen to paper in your outdoor sanctuary. Thank you. God has fashioned in us a true friendship and sisterhood.

Beryl Henne, my first editor, I admire you for asking, "So when are you going to finish the book?" True to form, I snapped, "When you decide to edit it!" You edited your way through the spits and spurts of brain spillage after Edith dissected and typed out the handwritten beginnings. Your hours of hard work crafted the beginning of this work.

Winning the 2019 Word Alive Press Free Publishing Contest for Non-Fiction meant my story would become the book God had promised. Publisher Jen Jandavs-Hedlin, you read the shmattah of handwritten binders somewhere around 2008, encouraged me to keep writing, and held those words in your heart. Thank you. Yours is a fearless, dedicated team I've come to know as Tia Friesen, project manager, and Kerry Wilson, editor. If this book is meant to shine, you have made it possible.

Words are inadequate when I think about how to thank my family. Since 1999 we have grown in number into a family knit together because we all matter, we all have value, and we all show and tell this to each other regularly.

My grandbabies, tiny and tall, I love you meeces to pieces and like crazy!

Wilma, you fell into my heart and stayed there. In you, God has given me another daughter to love on. Your selflessness encircles me with hope.

Murray, you pursue God's heart for yourself and everyone else … besides, who doesn't love a son-in-law who's also a techie!

To my son, Aaron: Your eyes have always spoken without spoken words. When the mom you had known faded, you steadfastly supported and loved the different me God designed. I love you a bushel and a peck.

To my precious Andrea, who had a vivacious mom one day and not the next. During your personal upheavals of that loss, you helped me in kazillion ways. With tender touches you taught me to become a gracious receiver. You believed I still had unsung songs in my heart, and that one day I'd get to sing them. I felt safe with you then and now. Hey, pretty girl, loving you is easy.

My Don, husband, and beloved faithful friend, only you come the closest to knowing how painful and long this journey has been. We've walked through the great loss and sadness as well as the joyful gain of love together for over forty-seven years. No doubt about it, this book would not exist or have been completed had you not made provision around every corner, over hill and dale, and during the last leg! Thank you. How I love the way you respond to the nudges of the Holy Spirit. Everyone should have a Donnie in their life! I get to love you here on earth and for all eternity.

Abba, my Heavenly Father, I love You. I just do! I have trusted, obeyed, and now honour You by having finished what you gave me to do. Use this book as you will, it's yours. Along the way you have brought me through the consuming fire of your love and at times I wanted out, but your Holy Spirit never ever left me through it all. Thank you. May those who read these pages know Truth. There is a real place inside you call "Courage." You lead the way to show us all where to look.

Foreword

by August H. Konkel, Ph.D

There's a Place Deep inside Called Courage will take readers to places most have never gone. Since the time of the so-called Enlightenment, there has been a tendency in the Western world to limit knowledge to the universe perceived by the senses. As Hedy Wiebe tells her story, the reader will enter another world ancient Hebrews knew as the realm of the holy. They practised the intersection of these worlds in all daily actions. The priests' task is to distinguish between "the holy and the common" (Leviticus 10:10). The holy is the source of life in the common. Western thinking that believes life is somehow inherent within the common is ultimately doomed to the loss of life. Wiebe points us to the source of life.

While the Hebrews expressed the dimension of the holy in temple symbols, they also encountered it in experience. Hedy Wiebe describes experience outside the common in what she calls "the grey zone." No one can choose to enter this zone, nor would anyone choose to do so voluntarily. But one fateful day in July of 1999, Hedy found herself in that zone. It was her encounter with the holy that enabled her to survive the ravages and pain of a body torn apart in a car collision. It was a world that included personal encounters with angels and seeing the presence of Jesus—the world of the holy made possible for her life in the world of the common.

One does not take a casual walk into the world of the holy. It takes courage to survive such a journey. It is not a safe place. It involves much suffering of the kind most of us hope never to need to understand, both physical and mental. One of the great mysteries of life given by the holy is the mental, which is both the greatest of blessings and, as Hedy explains, can also be utterly distressing. What is the function of brain in relation to mind? Why is the mind rendered handicapped by injury to the brain? Brain injury is perhaps the most distressing of all bodily injuries. Because of brain injury, others can no longer perceive the person of the mind, the person trapped inside the injured brain. Hedy's experience is a must-read in a day dominated by mental illness and concussions. Do not speak tritely with those of injured brain, because they know they are still the person of a healthy mind.

Perhaps it's the willful limitation of knowledge to the universe of the common that the Western world does not know how to deal with pain and death, other than to try to deny it or escape it. This includes well-meaning Christians who have no idea how to respond to those in suffering bodies, including an injured brain. This book is a must-read to learn a little more of what not to do or say in situations almost everyone encounters daily in some fashion.

Mostly, Hedy's story must be read because it's an inspiration to live. Few of us will need to struggle to get to a locked door in a stubborn wheelchair, only to encounter an angry, profanity- driven homecare worker who is potentially dangerous to a handicapped person. Courage for such vulnerable situations is more than what is ever demanded for more ordinary-stress-driven lives.

This book will make the reader a better person. It's another introduction to the reality of the holy and the foundation of life. It's a lesson on courage for how to live life, for life is never a safe place.

August H. Konkel, Ph.D.
Professor of Old Testament
McMaster Divinity College, Hamilton, ON
Past President of Providence University College
and Theological Seminary

A Letter from
Dr. Ian Mogilevsky

Hedy has written an extraordinary book. This is not surprising, since she is an extraordinary person who's had an extraordinary life! This book is a raw and honest account of her experience in a traumatic motor vehicle accident (MVA) and the years that followed. Her narrative describes the physical, emotional, relational, and spiritual struggles she experienced after her MVA. She takes the reader on a journey into the dark and hidden places that exist within all of us. There she meets her Lord, who graciously provides His presence and holds her in "His keeping."

Hedy's Christian faith is deep—deep from experienced trauma and loss, and deep from a continuous reliance on the Lord through her trauma and recovery. From her heart, she carefully portrays her personal experience of being in an MVA, her spiritual transformation, and what she discovered about God's presence, power, and faithfulness in her life. Hedy provides a stirring and vivid account. You will be guided into her reality, and you will be changed. Her testimony will at times bring tears to your eyes, and at other times a smile to your face. She describes her necessary dependency in her Lord during the days, weeks, and months after her MVA, which has continued throughout the years. Her transformation by God is clearly evident within these pages.

Throughout her book, she will point you to her God, who is loving, faithful, and kind. You will be inspired to live your life in the way that is totally surrendered to God and worthy of the calling you have received.

Dr. Ian Mogilevsky, Ph.D.
Registered Psychologist
Listed with the Psychological Association of Manitoba (PAM)

The Beginning

In His Keeping

"Call to me and I will answer you and tell you great and unsearch-
able things you do not know."

—Jeremiah 33:3, NIV

These words are as true and real to me as the fact that my life as I knew it
stopped the day I was injured in the crash. The high-impact trauma had left
me immediately unconscious with no memory of the actual events. What
had really happened to me—the "me" who was barely alive? That's the "me"
who will be alive for all eternity when I step into heaven one day and get
to stay there.

Several years into my recovery, I was experiencing pain associat-
ed with every aspect of the work of getting well-er-er. I was beginning to
emerge from survival mode and was wondering about the accident itself.
I'd been able to piece together events from the official police report and
what I'd been told by my family, doctors, and friend. I'd read the Manitoba
Public Insurance version, and spoke with my occupational, physical, and
vestibular therapists. Still, I had no memory of my own.

One neurologist grinned as he leaned back in his chair during yet another required assessment. His kind eyes spoke as clearly as his words as
he relayed the following explanation, as I remember it: "Organic amnesia
is both a blessing and a curse. Being unconscious right away means your
brain didn't log in what happened. That's why you don't always wake up
screaming or jolting awake because of nightmares about the accident. Your
brain has nothing in there to remember. That's the blessing. The curse is in

the confusion you feel. It's like looking at a blank wall. Your brain knows there's something on it … it just doesn't know what it is."

Together we laughed about having a legitimate reason for being a scatterbrain, or putting words together that made absolutely no sense. I asked him if I would always be like that and he laughed out loud! I was furious, but then he said, "At least you know how to be mad. That's good. Your brain will eventually figure out more, and in about five years, you'll know what will come back and what won't."

"Well," I retorted, annoyed, "that helps me like a hole in the head! *And…*," I continued, raising my voice, "people look at me funny when I speak, *and* I didn't even know that *what* I said made no sense! *And* I see their mouths move when they speak, but I haven't a clue *what* they said. I hear the voice, but for all I know, they're speaking Greek or Spanish into a funnel where nothing makes sense! *And* I hate stuttering!"

He continued to smile and said, "Well, Hedy, you didn't stutter today! You're so highly verbal, you'll fool most people most of the time! Keep practising and eventually you'll get it right."

Eyes twinkling, he checked something on his paper and grinned again. "You're actually off the charts in the 'highly verbal' category. Keep your sense of humour and your ability to laugh at yourself. You'll be able to see how much better you are in a few years."

"Finally!" I grinned back. "After all these years, my mouth will be good for something!"

I left his office that day and asked Jesus to make my words my best asset and make them useful. Rather cheekily, I told Him it would have to be up to Him.

* * *

Soon after that appointment, my wondering led me down a familiar path—time set apart to talk with my Father, my heavenly one. Just us. Alone. We'd talk about whatever was on my heart. These were incredibly safe times when I felt completely physically wrapped in unconditional love. A holy bubble. Sometimes I felt a breeze brush my face when I knew there was no physical wind. I felt whole and, in those moments, pain free. I'd tell or ask my friend anything.

I'd gotten to know God the Father, God the Son, and God the Holy Spirit as the One they truly are. We'd talk. Those were holy, special times. Since the accident, I'd learned to recognize His voice, and when He spoke, I'd listen. When I was finally able to hold a pencil, I'd often jot down words of His loving ways to me. I now heard differently than in the twenty-some years before. I paid close attention in my spirit.

Courage rose up, pushing me to ask a question that had swirled around and been dismissed in my thoughts many times. This day, however, became different. I asked, "Abba, I'm wondering … may I know what really happened to me? You were there, and you know."

What happened next resulted in one of my most intimate times with my Lord. Tears flowed with gratitude when I heard Him speak deep within. Grabbing a pen and paper, I began writing. I heard His voice inside and throughout myself. He spoke; I wrote. I'd take breaks and His voice would stop. As soon as I'd sit down again, the voice of my Keeper would continue to speak where He'd left off. He spoke and I recorded. He stopped and I took a break. But every time I sat down with pen and paper in hand, the presence of the Holy Spirit would descend and cover me as I listened and wrote. Awareness of God's holy presence had been with me every moment since the accident. He led. I obeyed. I asked. He answered me. After about three days, Abba stopped speaking. His loving warmth intensified. Humbled, yet wordless and thankful, I crawled into bed, tucked up the comforter, and silently wept on my pillow. Exhausted, I slept.

* * *

"I am the good shepherd; I know my own sheep, and they know me"
—John 10:14

Nothing in my life could have prepared me for that encounter with God or the aftermath of living in the wake of high-impact trauma. How does anyone prepare for life turning on a dime? Impossible! One doesn't. I sure hadn't! But it is possible to choose to believe and get to know God's ever-present presence during the mess … or not. I chose to believe—again, and again, and yet again.

This precious time was surreal. I wanted to be selfish and keep His words to me for myself, but He said not to. I deliberately put what God said to me in the beginning of this life story because the way He communicated was crystal clear.

"'*Eye has not seen, nor ear heard, nor have entered into the heart of man the things which God has prepared for those who love him.' But God has revealed them to us through His* Spirit" (1 Corinthians 9–10a, NKJV). These are words from His Word that my Keeper has lovingly repeated to me so I could continue to live in courage and leave behind that place of utter devastation. These words helped me heal during the nitty gritty work of continual rehab and to learn to live in that place of joy-filled restoration here on the earth. There really is a place deep inside called "Courage."

> *The gatekeeper opens the gate for him, and the sheep recognize his voice and come to him. He calls his own sheep by name and leads them out. After he has gathered his own flock, he walks ahead of them, and they follow him because they know his voice. They won't follow a stranger; they will run from him because they don't know his voice.*
>
> —John 10:3–5

* * *

Come, I will show you. I will show you a secret. Take My hand. Come this way. I want to show you something.

Your hand fits in Mine. It fits just fine. Here, let Me lead you over to where you can see while I hold you. See what I see? It's the fullness of life. It's the breath from My heart.

It is enough that I see; you do not need to. It is enough that I see quietness and strength, and I will help you see what I see. It is from this vantage point that I wait for you to come to Me. I'm your Father. Come sit with Me so I can tell you what is next. I know. Don't fret or be nervous. Just come into the living room of My heart. Welcome. Now let's talk. You listen.

You know how much I have taught you Myself. My joy is complete, for you have come to Me through My only Son, whose complete love brought you here to Me so that I can tell you what you need to know. Write of how My love, My courage, My hope flowed into your body, mind, and soul at the moment of impact.

You needed Me differently then than you'd ever needed Me before. You flew into My keeping. I am the Keeper you needed. All people need My keeping, but that day as you were unmercifully being forced into unnatural positions that broke so much of your precious body, broke and erased so much of your beautiful mind, My truth prevailed as it always does. Your spirit was free to leap fully into Mine. I released all of Heaven's keeping upon you. Did you know I was in the car too? I was. Come, let Me lead you and tell you how it really was that day in the car.

I felt the damage to your body as the airbag hit your face. I saw the damage as your brain moved and your inner ear crystals floated out of place. I knew the long road of recovery for you as I held your head in that unnatural angle as your body moved with the force of destruction. I felt your bones snap and break as your ankles were pushed sideways until they could no longer stay as I had once created them to be. I knew the courage you would need to learn to walk again. I gave you My courage in that moment, for I knew you would need Me like that forever.

As your body flung forward and the seatbelt held tight, I welcomed you as your ribs cracked and your spine stretched, becoming so bruised. I winced and cried out without restraint as your arm muscles and tendons ripped and ligaments tore. Your suffering fell into Me as I fell into you. Your need for Me was great that day. I was right in you as the blunt force of airbag and dashboard hit your stomach, created havoc in your pancreas, spleen, and colon. Those things I created to work perfectly were being destroyed, and the tears inside began to bleed. The blood I meant to sustain you was turning on itself to destroy you. I held you as you bled in places I designed to be knit together when I created you in your momma's womb.

I AM the Peace you, my daughter, and your friend felt as you tumbled, twisted, and rolled. I AM the Presence she saw and felt as you both became broken.

I wept, as I knew that the voice you used to sing, pray, and praise Me was being taken from you. As your Father, I held your helpless body. Did you know I AM the puff of wind you felt on your face for just a breath's moment as your mind engaged briefly with the reality of pain in this world? Did you know that I AM what you now call the "grey place," where I placed you when your body couldn't stand the pain in your flesh?

I AM the Word of the Spirit, and I hovered in, through, and over you. I never left. Never. I have always stayed. In those moments as your mind drifted in and out, your spirit acknowledged my indwelling Holy Spirit. My Father's heart for you rejoiced because you had come and been welcomed into Me on December 20, 1975. Yes, I remember. It was at 2:21 on that Sunday afternoon. The time and date are important to you, My child, for I know everything.

I assured you, My daughter, and your friend that I am God. I held her and you, and used those willing to come help you.

The glowing light they saw was My light because My hands held secure as willing hearts came to help.

Years before, you asked Me to let your life be a reflection of Me. A picture of Me. I answered by showing My light to those who came to help you. As they worked hard to get you out of the mangled mess of metal, it was My love that led them all. I knew you would need to see and hear Me, so I let you see My face in the light, hear Me in the language I taught you, feel Me in the wind, and smell My fragrance all the time. Such intimate love is for you, so I caused you to remember Me in each moment of pain as torment ripped through your body. It broke like the porcelain vase I had taught you about. Because I am Goodness, My tender mercy cradled your broken body, your resting mind, and your spirit, which was very much alive. You had to know Me as truly One.

With the fruit of My Holy Spirit's infilling pouring from your voice box, I caught each sound and snatched it from the air as Mine. Each utterance, every cry, all moans came straight to Me for safe keeping. You were about to know Me as Keeper, so I breathed that breath of air you felt on your left ear. Yes, you knew Me instantly. In that instant, I withheld you from earthly death as I spoke: "Hedy, I will keep you."

The darkness of the deep was near as you felt fear crawl up the skin on your toes and begin the death grip on your heart. I, the sovereign Lord, rose up and rescued you from fear as you opened your eyes and recognized the round ceiling light in the ambulance. I opened the heavens for you to see the myriad—yes, a myriad—of beautiful beings you call the angelic host. They are always waiting to welcome My children home. All of heaven hovered and waited for Me. I have not given you descriptive words for all you saw, but instantly you knew Me completely as I already know you.

With one breath I blew the useless chaff from your life and sent the two angels you saw, who instantly dispelled fear from your mind and body. They, huge as they are, were commanded to fit in that ambulance corner, and willingly they kept vigilant watch over you. They already know that my keeping is the same on earth as it is in heaven. You were to know that later. They never once left you alone. They held the darkness at bay as many servant hearts and hands moved quickly. I guided their thoughts to help you.

On the earth they saw a mangled mess. I saw you. You saw Me in the liquid-gold hues everywhere and in the first eyes you remember. She was the beautiful nurse whose voice drew your mind to remember your own name.

No one else knew that the unconscious language in your spirit was calling to come home. That's what I created you for—to come home. Even then you longed for Me and knew Me. I stayed close in the place where we fellowshipped and talked Spirit to spirit. I loved hearing your pure, childlike babbling. It was then that the river of My life flowed freely. I illuminated My light onto your seeing heart. I knew you could hear and know Me there and there alone. I spoke often as I do now. My sheep hear My voice.

The hard board you were strapped to added to your pain, but there was no other way the well-trained medics knew to move you. Mercifully, I held you as those brave paramedics sawed and grinded the car's metal away from you. Your ears were closed to the sounds of the Jaws of Life I showed them to use to get you out and onto the hard slab. The first tears you saw were my tears as I used that young doctor's eyes to show you My love. I wept because you hurt. I wept healing tears for you through those who first saw you at the scene, in the ambulance, and at the hospital.

I also let righteous anger against this awful injustice propel several medics and doctors to fight for your life. I used them because they invited

Me in. You did not hear their silent cries of "O God! O God help me! Help me now!" I answered those cries for you.

It was Me you saw holding your husband, Don, as he saw your face. I held him close as all reason left him and rage took over. Love had already won his heart, and he was free to feel.

My child, your daughter Andrea was so afraid. So very afraid. It was raw fear you saw in Andrea's eyes. I held the fear and her at the same time. She knew my presence and cried out to Me. My angels held her close, as was their given task. Other angels were assigned other tasks. That is why each time your eyes opened to all of heaven at your disposal, you saw much light, which allowed you to see Me inside some people, around others, next to others, and not near others at all. I, however, used all, for all is at My disposal. I will and do use anything all the time.

I purposely held you close to Me, so close that you could smell Me. As you now know, My fragrance is unlike anything you smell on earth. The sweet aroma is Mine. You often fell into my scent and were safe there. I filled your senses in the Spirit with Myself, for I knew you'd know Me in the fragrance.

I had Wilma, your son Aaron's sweet fiancée, wash her hair earlier that day so that when she bent to touch you, her hair caressed your swollen face. The fragrance of her shampooed hair let you connect with love here on earth. Although she did not know it at the time, she came in Me and gave to you My fragrance. Now you have come to Me, and your words will bring My fragrance to those who need to know My scent.

As you write now, there are those who will not believe I am always speaking. I am. You have simply chosen to obey Me, trust Me, and write down what you are hearing with your spirit-friendly, attentive ears. Faith is really quite simple and child-like. You have chosen to believe.

I AM simply who I say that I AM. Simply simple. You learned to hear My voice, and you responded in your child-like simple faith of knowing Me as you chattered in that other tongue while the red light in the CT scanner blinked. I had all of you fall into Me when you needed to be moved to be examined, so that those who know how I created your body could make accurate assessments with the information the tests gave them.

Mary Magdalene did not recognize Me at first either, but I set her body free from her accusers. Then she came to Me, and I set her spirit free. Yet even after the cross, she did not recognize Me until I called her name: "*Mary*" (John 20:16). It is not unusual for My created ones to not recognize Me, even when they look for Me.

I am really the light of the world, and in Me there is no darkness. That is why you saw none. The truth is, you could see My light. Really. My all-consuming light, My glory, literally covered everything you saw every time your eyes opened. Your spirit, being alive in Me, knew only one thing: response to Me.

I am Mercy, Wisdom, and Knowledge. For a moment I physically let you see young Dr. B., who led the Gold Service Team at the Health Sciences Centre. My heart moved with compassion upon you both. I let you see who I saw—a young man desperate to save your life and not make an error in judgement. I answered your request to not let him live with the guilt of making a mistake. I caused him to hear Me say "wait" as he deliberated whether to cut you open as your abdomen continued to swell. My compassion for you overwhelmed him, causing him to know that he needed to simply wait.

The angels you saw in the ambulance had escorted you into that step-down room, one at the head of your bed, and the other at your feet. They were there to guarantee the safety of your soul. The wonderful way I had intended for your body and mind to work had been devastated by your world and the choice of another. You have no language to help you describe continuous, torturous pain. You remember how awful it was even now. I was present when your pancreas reached dangerously distended levels. I hovered as your kidneys struggled to function. I held your heart as it fought to keep pumping blood. With every breath passing through your windpipe, I was pushing life into your bruised lungs. I waited in agony as your gut filled with body fluids never designed by Me to flow there. Bile was suffocating you, yet I did not let the doctor decide to cut you open to relieve the pressure. Instead, I answered the prayers of hope by having you spill out the toxic fluid. I rejoiced as the cheer came forth among the doctors and nurses when you vomited the vile orange bile from yourself. I laughed with them as they laughed with relief. Some recognized My hand and witnessed the miracle before them. Others saw only the mess and what they would have to do to clean it up. But for those who believed, it was a time to dance in My Spirit as I once again relieved you into the unconscious grey place of not knowing or feeling anything—only Me, all of Me, as you've come to know Me. Three in One. I truly am the one true God of all. I had blown away everything in your life that you would not need to live, and I had prepared all you would need to live.

Hedy, as you write now, you wonder if it is really My voice you hear or just what you remember being told or your imagination. To all I tell you, yes, yes, and yes. I abide in you, and you abide in Me. I tell you in my living Word that you are in Me, in Christ. What others think of this is My business with them. You hear Me and write what you hear so that others will believe and know I am who I say that I am. I am alive. I am alive in you, and I speak so you can hear with the "ears of your heart." Hedy, you needed to know Me in that place of utter devastation in your human mind and body. You need to know Me today. Be still and listen; be assured and write what I impress upon your heart and mind.

As you lay there, tubes and medical apparatus were attached to record every moment, breath, and change in the midst of the flurry of activity from doctors and nurses rushing to save your body's life. I heard the cry of your friend and My daughter, Wendy. My dear child, you are to know I heard every desperate cry. "Death, you can't have her! Stand back, Death. Jesus, save her!"

I responded to her cry as your belly distended, robbing your lungs of air and pushing them outward toward the broken ribs. My timing is always timely. In that moment, My glory fell as your body spewed forth the fluids building in it. All you saw was an orange mess, but others saw the colours of my rescue. I gave you to the doctor, for I trusted him with you. The prayers of the righteous avail much. Wendy needed to know that I had answered her frantic need for Me alone to save. She and others moved My hand of compassion for you. They knew not the extent of your injuries. I alone knew that in the days that were yet to come, many whom I love would have despaired unless they believed they would see My goodness right in front of them, *"in the land of the living"* (Psalm 27:13, NASB).

Human ears heard your painful moaning. Those who loved you wept as they saw what the blow from the airbag had done to your head and face. I saw the horror and held them all. I loved you as dearest Donna moved to soothe you as you cried out in wailing pain, her loving dips of water to your mouth really were given in My name. Did you know she sang praises, thankful she could be near you? She always smells so good, doesn't she? Her fragrance was the perfume you smelled as you slept. My fragrance, as you know, is quite different, even more lovely than human love. Smelling Me assured you of being in Me. Smelling Donna, Wilma, and Andrea let you know you were alive. Andrea was alone, so I sent Wendy and Donna. Don was so afraid and lost that I sent Pastor Todd. Aaron had Wilma to hold him. Don and Andrea had not yet learned to comfort each other with My comfort. I held them and you all in My heart, for in My keeping you would heal. While your mind and body writhed and struggled with involuntary movements pain induces, your spirit moved freely in Me, for you are forever alive in Me. I showed you that your spirit will never die. I in you, and you in Me.

I AM amazing. I AM God. As you sense My presence know this: I am near you. There is My Word of assurance today, the same as then.

> *This command I am giving you today is not too difficult for you, and it is not beyond your reach. It is not kept in heaven, so distant that you must ask, 'Who will go up to heaven and bring it down so we can hear and obey?' It is not kept beyond the sea, so far away that you must ask, 'Who will cross the sea to bring it to us so we can hear it and obey?' No, the message is very close at hand; it is on your lips and in your heart so that you can obey it.*
>
> —Deuteronomy 30:11–14

I, the Lord your God, speak. I spoke this, and I will always speak.

In those moments that turned into hours, then days, and then lengthened to months, I saw you. I saw *you*. Others saw a broken you, but I saw *you*. I, Jesus your friend, became Courage— Courage so you could be well. I bathed you in the tears you shed when you were alone with Me. I used them to heal you. It would take years for your body and mind to respond and obey My healing touches. I, as Courage, strengthened your resolve to fight. Fight to be well.

Hedy, tell others that when there is nothing left to lose, when you've lost all that matters, I begin. I will begin what matters to Me. You. Because you matter to Me.

I began to give you courage to believe Me. I would be hope so that you could live in the joy My hope gives. Healing began the moment you emptied the contents of your belly all over the doctors, nurses, bed, and floor, but only I knew. My restoration would follow in the years to come— because I alone have numbered your days on the earth. I alone, for I am still the Beginning and the End.

So now say "Amen."

* * *

I trembled inside when I heard all this; my lips quivered with fear. My legs gave way beneath me, and I shook in terror. I will wait quietly for the coming day when disaster will strike the people who invade us. Even though the fig trees have no blossoms, and there are no grapes on the vine; even though the olive crop fails, and the fields lie empty and barren; even though the flocks die in the fields, and the cattle barns are empty, yet I will rejoice in the Lord! I will be joyful in the God of my salvation! The Sovereign Lord is my strength! He will make me as surefooted as a deer, able to tread upon the heights.
—Habakkuk 3:16–19

Thank you, Abba. I understand. I will try to tell my story, because I promised you I would. You gave me the title and said it would someday be a book.

CHAPTER
One

It happened on a Thursday. The day was sunny and hot, just the way I liked a summer day to be. Great tanning weather! My recently-retired husband, Don, on the other hand, was sweating buckets as he battled with the fact that years of weathering had wreaked havoc on the cedar fence around our property in Winnipeg, Manitoba. He had years of practice doing battle under his belt, even with an ornery fence. After twenty-seven years of service in the Winnipeg Police Service, that fence was a "piece of cake," or as they say, a sweaty "walk in the park." He was vigorously scrubbing and bleaching those boards surrounding our yard, preparing them to be stained. The fence desperately needed attention.

I, on the other hand, had been lazily tanning on a lounge but had gone inside and stood in the kitchen, contemplating what to make for supper. I was undecided. Making meals in our home was often a family affair.

Our twenty-one-year-old son, Aaron, wouldn't be home for dinner. He was working long hours at his job during the Pan American Games in our city that summer. His responsibilities included overseeing and coordinating the sound and technical systems needed to take care of thirty-five athletic events hosted at twenty-eight different venues. Between working, planning his wedding to a blue-eyed, brown-haired beauty, Wilma, trying to chat with him was like trying to catch the back end of a fish!

I heard our daughter, Andrea. At seventeen, she had just graduated from high school the month before and was somewhere in the house. She may very well have been at her beloved keyboard playing songs as she sang (or rather belted out) any number of tunes. At random, she'd switch between jazz riffs to worship choruses, or fiddle around creating new songs with complete freedom—wherever the music inside led her. I loved listening, especially when she thought nobody else was around. Andrea being herself always made me smile … still does.

Our phone rang that afternoon on July 31, 1999, around 3:50 pm. A long-time friend was calling to ask if I wanted to go for a ride up to Gimli. She'd forgotten to crank down the air vent on the top of her trailer in the RV campground near Gimli Beach.

I was more than game. We decided to have supper at the Seagull Restaurant, eat outside, and watch the waves lap on the beach. No time for the usual tanning we often did together—just zip out for the hour it would take, have supper, and be back before dark. The plan was to have a bit of girlfriend fun time.

I called out to Don to tell him where we were going. He didn't mind. He was wonderfully busy, messy, and happy. Ten minutes later, I hollered my goodbyes over my shoulder to Andrea, assuming those two would find something to eat or would pick up a pizza for their dinner.

By four o'clock, my friend had pulled up in front of our home in her brand-new turquoise-blue Neon. I slid into the passenger side and belted in as always, sliding the strap under my right armpit away from its annoying irritation. I hated the belt rubbing against my neck. I positioned myself slightly to the left, facing her as she drove.

I automatically sat sideways in her car so she could not only hear better but read my lips and facial expressions. She never missed much. She noticed detail and read most people really well. Feeling happy, we left, laughing at the fact that it was a great excuse not to cook but to have supper at the lake, where she'd have company rather than having to go there and back by herself.

We engaged in the usual "girl chatter" as we headed north on Henderson Highway, hung a left onto the Perimeter Highway that surrounds Winnipeg, and then right onto Main Street. Going north past Middle Church and onto Highway 8, we joined the rush hour traffic. Lots of traffic going north. Lots going home after work to Selkirk, Lockport, and Gimli.

Highway 8 has two lanes going north and two lanes going south, with a wide, grassy median-type ditch in the middle. There are several major intersections, some with lights, others with stop or merge signs to direct oncoming traffic, enabling continuous flow onto Highway 8.

The highway speed is one hundred klicks. Traffic moved smoothly that day, with slower-moving vehicles on the right and numerous cars in the left lane passing the cars slowing down to turn right onto McPhillips toward Selkirk. A large McDermott lumber truck was one such vehicle on Highway 8. The male driver of the truck noticed a maroon van zipping around the bend on McPhillips, travelling toward the highway. The van moved quickly and should have been slowing to stop at the Highway 8 intersection.

The truck driver realized that the van was not slowing for the stop sign but instead was going to try to beat the highway traffic going north, crossing over right in front of him. He could see a female driver as he braked to slow his big lumber truck.

On his left, however, vehicles passed him at the usual speed, completely oblivious of the oncoming danger, since his long transport truck blocked all view of the intersection and the speeding van. He could do nothing for those vehicles passing him.

Helpless, he watched as a little blue Neon zipped past him. The maroon van had by then run the stop sign. Horrified, he and others in north and southbound lanes watched as the Neon T-boned the van, smashing right behind the driver's side as it came across the highway. He knew there was no time for the driver of the little car to swerve or brake.

The collision caused direct front impact to the driver's side of the van and a head-on, full- speed hit for the Neon. People in other cars and trucks slammed on their brakes, swerving to miss the Neon and van as both began careening and rolling into the grassy median. Many watched in horror as the Neon flipped numerous times, with glass flying and metal making an awful, freakish noise. The van flipped and rolled into the grassy ditch. Had it rolled much farther, it would have gone from crossing two lanes of northbound traffic and into two lanes of oncoming southbound traffic. Fortunately, it stopped rolling as it came up out of the incline of the ditch, landing on its four wheels!

A young mother and her four-year-old child were inside the van. The child had not been buckled in as the law required. The mom had disobeyed the law by not stopping at the stop sign on McPhillips and Highway 8. She had been preoccupied with her child and made a very bad mistake. That careless mistake caused our accident.

Our Neon had pitched and rolled, finally stopping by crashing down hard onto its roof, pinning us both inside. The airbags deployed as the windows burst into shreds, shards flying outward and inward. The mangled car was inches from the only light pole in the middle ditch. All this had occurred around the "S" curve close to the bend near the St. Andrews Airport.

The collision produced a flurry of activity among the people in the other vehicles on Highway 8. We were told later that one man at the scene, an off-duty police officer, saw it all happen. His years of training, quick response, and skill kicked into gear. He had his cell phone and used it to call 911. I never found out who that first officer was, but if ever he finds the words on this page, this is what he would hear me say in my letter to him:

> Dear Now-Yet-Nameless,
> Did you know you were there not by chance? Do you know you were handpicked by my Sovereign God to be right there with eyes to see, a clear-thinking mind, and specially designed abilities to help me that day?
>
> Thank you for responding and not driving by. Thank you for not saying, "Let somebody else deal with this mess."
>
> You made the first call that participated with all of heaven. It was how my God intended to help me, His child, who was being wounded. You apparently knew whom to call, and the Selkirk detachment of the RCMP came.
>
> You were first on the scene, I'm told. You were able to provide a full report. Thank you for that, because it was especially important to my husband, Don, a fellow police officer. He needed to know exactly how and what had happened to me.
>
> I want you to know I have a vague sense, just a faint inkling, of a man's kind eyes peering at me from somewhere. I have often wondered if that was you. Thank you, dear Now-Yet-Nameless-One, for doing what you did for me.
>
> If someday we meet here on earth, I know that I'll know you instantly, because I continue to hold you in my heart with gratitude and thanksgiving. I will recognize your eyes.

My favorite Bible verse says it well, "*I thank my God upon every remembrance of you*" (Philippians 1:3, NKJV).

If ever we meet in heaven, it will be God's business to decide how we recognize one another.

Live ever so blessed,

The unconscious lady in the mangled wreck,

Hedy Wiebe

Severe trauma to the gut; ankles broken sideways with bilateral breaks; snapped ribs; multiple rips and tears; muscles and tendons forced, stretched, and torn into unnatural places in my face; rotated hips, arms, shoulders, and back; and a whack to the head, called sheering to the brain, give new meaning to feeling of being "run over by a truck." My first memory after that impact spells one word: *pain!* Excruciating pain! However, the second thing I remember is what I really want to tell you about.

Many years earlier, I had been introduced to the Lord and the Bible, and Jesus had caused my spirit to be born again so that His Holy Spirit could live there. No wonder that my primary form of communicating with God was a continuation of His Spirit to my spirit. I heard the language of my spirit as I heard the sound of my voice. Conscious or unconscious, every moment was filled with incredible, indescribable, searing pain, but piercing through that was stillness and peace. I existed in what I call the "grey place" but lived completely in a spiritual realm that's not usually visible here on earth. I was alert there.

At first after impact there was no sense of danger—no sense of time. There was only one way to be: either here on earth or in heaven. I couldn't even choose. Not then. I simply was in a place where there was no confusion, no mystery, no confounding intellect or logic to be a bother—just a simple knowing of Truth. While medical trauma people did what they do, I heard a siren. I was forced back to a searing awareness of pain and then abruptly faced a blinding, probing light. I looked up to a ceiling light in an ambulance. Immediately, I saw the heavens open, and I knew I was seeing a myriad of angels. Their movement was constant and there was no end to them. They weren't looking down at me but all faced in one accord toward their Creator. It was a not-to-be-described kind of beautiful movement bathed entirely in liquid-golden light. In response to such beauty, I responded out of the innermost part of me. Up through my distending gut, through my throat, I heard the familiar, strange-sounding syllabic utterances of my spirit. Time didn't exist. There was no conscious, earthly thinking.

Jarred from that place back to where only excruciating pain screamed, I heard a male voice say, "We're losing her. Trach her."

A different male voice by my head said, "I'm having trouble here! You need to stop babbling now, ma'am."

I did and went back where all was grey.

Next, I felt something awful crawling by my feet, up my calves, onto my thighs, and toward my hands. I opened my eyes to see what it was, but instead I saw two angels leaning casually toward each other. They completely filled the right corner of the ambulance, floor to ceiling. They seemed to be waiting for their orders. They were huge and white.

Instantly, I became aware of a fear that had begun to descend, making itself known to me. The crawling feeling intensified. It felt heavy. Somehow, I knew I was in danger. It was hard to breathe. I became aware of those huge two angels once more. The second I saw them leaning near my feet, all the effects fear had on my body disappeared. Instantly gone! It never returned.

I glanced to my left and briefly saw a man sitting there in hospital staff greens (fatigues?). I heard, "She's awake."

Again, a complete submersion into pain that has no words. It intensified. My head hurt so badly. Something was hurting my head. But then I felt a physical puff of warm air softly blow on my left ear. I knew it was God. I also heard and recognized His audible voice as His breath gently touched my ear area. These are the words I heard: "Hedy, I will keep you."

I knew His voice instantly. All the fear had already left me. I was now in His keeping and was about to learn how to live there—live in the deep places in the Spirit where God truly is everywhere and everything and breathes His life. Did I know Him like that then? Nope. Not then, but I would.

Chapter
two

SURFACING TO A PHYSICALLY SEMI-CONSCIOUS PLACE EQUALLED searing, unrelenting pain. Everywhere. Unbeknown to me, I had been transferred by ambulance to the emergency unit at the Seven Oaks Hospital in Winnipeg and then to the ICU at the Health Sciences Centre, where doctors and nurses fight to save someone's life. No pain killers because of the concern for closed-head injury. Organized scrambling that happens in life and death situations. My recall includes intermittently hearing beeping sounds, footsteps, and different voices and seeing eyes. Don's eyes full of fear. Andrea's, terrified. Concerned, worried eyes. Probing eyes, and ones full of pity. Yet kind, compassionate eyes washed over me with sensations of being present somewhere.

Within a few days, I was transferred to the step-down unit. This time is still mostly an unrecallable blur with bits of perceived accuracy. Memories of repeated sensations float by. Pain. Pain and more pain. Seeing golden liquid flow over everything and bringing peace. The welcome grey place of nothingness, and sucking for air, which meant searing pain. Snippets of words from men and women. They weren't in agreement about the condition of my legs, ankles, and feet. Someone told me they couldn't make the pain stop yet because "we need you awake." I remember the colour white and seeing the dark silhouettes of several males at my feet. Beside them, females stood. They appeared ready to run. *But* behind all of them stood one huge angel covering them all in the golden bright light. Thankfully, mercy came and held me as I slipped away from physical reality into that light. The next time I awoke, my legs didn't hurt as badly. They were on something soft, and something else soft kept them from moving.

It felt like there was something heavy weighing down my eyes. I'd try to force them open, and when I did, a kind soul would speak and I'd hear, "Welcome back" or "Okay, she's back." Somewhere during conscious times, I know I saw Don's eyes. He was afraid. Andrea's face was wet with tears, and Aaron's hand touched my hand. I smelled Wilma's hair.

Later I'd find out that my stomach hurt like crazy because of the swelling in my gut and the broken ribs just millimetres away from puncturing the left lung.

Anything I did see was blurry and distorted. (No wonder! Since my glasses had been blown off my face, I couldn't see diddley-squat.) I was told that the hemorrhaging in my eyes contributed to the constant state of dizziness and nausea. Note that they said "contributed." My eyes ached constantly. Deep aching. Gratefully, I'd slip into that grey place, and then … nothing… until I'd wake up to the misery and it would begin again.

I was in a white, round tunnel with a blinking red light above me when I jolted awake to find my awfully hurting head strapped down on something. All of me had been frozen into an unmovable place! There was something in my throat, but I couldn't scream "MAKE IT STOP!" Blissfully, the grey fuzziness softly surrounded me, and I felt nothing—until I heard someone far away telling me to wake up. I didn't want to. The voice was insistent. It was coaxing me awake through the foggy, thick grey place. I eventually found kind eyes looking at me. She had an object in her hand, and stated, "I can finally give you something for the pain." And then there was nothing.

Being in step-down is still a mixture of unrecallable blur and bits of accurate information. Just repeated sensations of pain and more pain, golden liquid peace, the grey place, the nothingness, sucking for air, and more pain. It felt like my legs had been put on pillows and held there with something soft. When I awoke, the pain in my legs wasn't as great, but my stomach hurt. I can't describe that level of pain.

Since my glasses had been blown off my face, not only was I in pain every waking moment, but any movement made me dizzy and nauseous, and things were blurry and distorted. The hemorrhaging in the eyes contributed to that. The eyes ached constantly with a deep aching.

Chapter
Three

AROUND DAY FIVE OR SIX, I WAS MOVED FROM THE STEP-DOWN UNIT TO the trauma unit. *Somebody moved me*, I thought as I woke up and discovered that I was no longer in the room filled with liquid gold covering everything and everybody. Now I could see a curtain and a wall. A nurse came in and smiled wearily, looking totally exhausted. "Welcome back," she said, moving to an IV bag on a pole. "I've got something for the pain."

I needed to know her name. I asked and she told me. I asked her how many of "me" she had. She looked confused.

"How many like me?" I asked (or rather gasped), hearing for the first time a voice that sounded completely different than my own.

She looked at me with pity and sighed. "Eight. Eight like you in critical care."

"I'll ask Jesus to help you." I remember nothing after that. She may have smiled as the meds made the pain stop.

The next time I woke it was dark in the room, and I saw a different female nurse checking the IV pole. She was standing in Someone I knew well. I would recognize Jesus anywhere, because He had let me see Him many times in the realm of the supernatural place when I was not awake here on the earth. She was literally standing *in* Jesus. I knew she knew Him.

I rasped at her: "You're standing in Jesus, you know."

She looked down, smiled, and said, "Oh, you're awake. I didn't mean to wake you."

"You are standing in Jesus," I insisted. "You know Him and are in Him right now."

Again she smiled and asked, "Can you really see Him?"

"Yes," I answered. "You love Jesus too."

Jesus let her face glow with Himself as she answered. "Yes. Yes, I do. I know He will help you get well, and so will I. There are many people praying for you here at the hospital. The ER has been full of your church friends and family for days. There are praying techs, nurses, and doctors calling you a miracle."

She squeezed my fingers, and I felt the liquid warmth of God's presence flow over me in the form of medicine, and I slept.

The next time I became aware of my surroundings, it must have been early morning, because I saw light shining through the window. The meds had worn off, so I frantically tried to find the help button. I then heard my dear Don's footsteps coming down the hallway before I saw him. I also smelled him. He entered the room and cautiously poked his head around the corner of the curtain. He reeked of sweat from being outside, and his hand was sticky and covered with grass and dirt.

"I see they moved you from step-down. You're right across the hall from the nurses' station," he stated matter-of-factly, without a "hello" or "How are you?"

I watched as he grunted, "Good thing." He held up a pair of mangled glasses with only one lens. "Found them," he said. "I went back and found them for you."

We stared at each other, the broken glasses in his large hands. He looked as devastated as I felt. Love had propelled him to go to the crash site in search of them for me.

I watched as his body swam and merged and morphed from one being into four, and then everything swirled counter clockwise. I blinked, confused that what I saw were my legs and feet swimming back and forth on white pillows. The unstoppable heaviness and nausea descended. I couldn't seem to keep my eyes open long enough to focus. All I did was tremble uncontrollably. I didn't know where I was or how long I'd been there. I saw Don slip away, and I longed for the grey place where there was nothing.

When I woke, Don was still there, and this time his eyes filled with the tears of hopeless helplessness. We cried as he tried to touch and hug me somewhere that was unhurt.

Chapter
four

ON THE DAY I WAS MOVED TO THE TRAUMA UNIT, I WAS UNAWARE OF what was happening. All I knew was that I was alive. I didn't realize that I was in a bed with an IV stuck somewhere, a "Foley" bag with tubing and assorted "trimmings" had been inserted to help me urinate, and monitors beeped as nurses came and went regularly. I knew excruciating pain, and that was it! Being in a drug-induced state allowed me moments of oblivion. Press a button with the thumb and wait. Ahhhh! Purposeful footsteps. A nurse, a needle—oblivion! Wake up. Emerge from the cave of the grey place aware of pain and nausea. I repeated that endless cycle every time I reached consciousness.

At one point during the blur of time one day, I heard two voices. I recognized them! Before forcing my eyes open, I heard them talking. My older sister, Betty, came around the corner and into the curtained-off section of the room. The look on her face said it all. I was completely unaware of my looks. Apparently, what she saw wasn't too great. Don stood behind her looking helpless. She looked determined.

I was no longer in the step-down unit, where personnel never have time to do anything but clean off what they need to clean to save lives. Trauma unit staff takes care of the essentials of stabilizing a patient. My sister, however, has an amazing gift. She assesses messes! She is about action. It was not okay that I lay there in that sad state. She saw what she saw, but I saw relief, concern, compassion, and determined action in her beautiful green eyes. She said something to someone in the room about my hair and was rather indignant that there was still broken glass and dried, matted blood sticking to my scalp.

Next, I heard my Don agree to something she said. He'd been rooted beside my bed, totally helpless, not knowing how to help me. Now there was a plan. Finally, work he could do. Gentle, kind love poured out of every part of him toward me. (I hope I smiled at them … no memory here.)

"Hedy, Don and I are going to try and wash your hair," Betty informed me. She's an amazing, efficient, put-one-step-in-front-of-the-other-to-get-'er-done woman. To this beautiful woman, it was intolerable that I lay there with filthy hair, and she was about to figure out a way to get me washed up! Now that they knew there were no fractures in my neck or spine, they could move me a bit.

"Don, I'm sure there's a bucket somewhere. Fill it with warm water." Betty has always had a tone in her voice when there's a mess!

I heard the two kick into gear. Clash! Bang! "I'll ask the nurse where they keep it."

Silently, I screamed, *My head! No, don't touch my head!* But touch it they did, carefully, gently lifting this dizzy blonde's matted hair mess onto the contraption used to wash the hair of a patient in bed. As they lowered the upper part of my body down to a flat position, I begged to pass out and wake up when they were done! Pain in the company of never-ending rolling nausea—not my kind of party!

I can still feel the glass chunks coming out of where they'd been pressing into my scalp, and I can still hear the dirty bits clink as they fell into a basin.

My body knew new heights of pain and utter discomfort as Betty and Don moved me into a flat position, slightly tilting my head upwards. Imagine your head as a soccer ball half filled with water sloshing around while it's being kicked. That's what the inside of my brain felt like. I experienced instant nausea while my broken ribs protested vehemently, a previously intubated esophagus filled with phlegm, and a horribly bruised spinal cord and torn ligaments under the shoulders and armpits ripped in pain—nasty. That day I was introduced to how my body would feel every waking moment of every day for many seemingly endless months.

Breathing, just shallow, gasping breaths—that was my part as I felt Betty and Don work in sync while washing my hair. Betty's capable hands extended in love, probing my scalp, and Don ever so gently poured warm water as needed.

The roaring noise in my head subsided and the pain eased as the wonderful morphine shot kicked into gear while the calming effect of the warm water soothed me. The room once more slowed its spinning, and the ceiling tiles became squarish. Clink, clink, plop, splash.

"Glass. There's still more glass chunks in her hair!" Betty huffed, as she does when something is totally intolerable in her mind!

No wonder my head hurts, I thought, completely ignorant of what was yet to come.

More soothing warm water created a marvellous sensation. These two servant hearts had done it. Loving light fuelled my sight. It was kind of like what Jesus does with the surrendered soul in need of forgiveness and cleansing. It's often painful as He washes us clean, no matter what the condition of our soul, because of love.

Those two washed my blood-encrusted hair of glass pieces, gravel, and grass and then made it clean. Head flat and tilted back, I pretty much sucked wind, trembled, and rolled with the dizziness and nausea, feeling like it would never end.

Don's big hands gently cradled my head, and somewhere underneath stood the bucket holding dirty shampoo suds, old blood, and pieces of smashed car window glass and other debris.

The feeling of clean hair for the first time was worth the effort. I don't remember being combed, changed, or anything else. I do know love cared for me in this act. Gratitude still wells up within me toward Betty and my hubby. It manifests itself into a lump in my throat as I write and remember.

How does one who is barely alive get washed? Very carefully, and after a shot of some sort! But unfailing love, wrapped up in Betty and Don, found me.

Talk about knowing the significance of the fact that my Jesus knows each hair follicle on my head! *"And the very hairs on your head are all numbered"* (Matthew 10:30). Honest! They truly are! God sent Betty and Don to take care of what He held in His hands. He let them minister to me. I was yet to learn this new way of being loved and cared for as the days turned into weeks, then months, and eventually years.

That was my introduction to day one out of the step-down area, where everything had been bathed in liquid gold each time I surfaced to wakefulness. I was now down the hall in the trauma unit, lying in a bed. Medical people came and went to attend to my needs, such as IVs, shots, pokes, prods, tests, and other medical procedures. Eventually, the worst part was the nightmare of manoeuvring onto a bedpan.

Whatever needed to be done got done while in bed, supported somehow by medical staff while I trembled, my teeth chattered, my muscles and head shook, my eyes blinked, and my ears roared and rang, all while I fought nausea in the ever-present, everywhere pain. Sensations of endlessly falling backwards into nothingness became my daily nemesis.

"Father," I'd whisper, "Y-you s-said You w-would k-keep me. You promised. You did." And once more, as always, the Holy Spirit would cradle me like a baby. I could truly feel the physical arms of my Lord hold me as I'd drift off to that place where I was alive in the Spirit and alert. My mind and body didn't work. They were broken, but I lived in His Spirit, for He indwells me. From that place of being alive I could see Jesus all around some people. They moved while surrounded by Him. Some were outside of Him. If I were an artist, I could maybe sketch what that looked like, but sadly, I draw stick people—rather poorly, as a matter of fact!

Nothing in my life could have fully prepared me for the aftermath of this accident. How does anyone prepare for their life to totally stop as they know it. They don't. They can only know God's presence in the midst. I did.

Chapter
five

FROM MY HOSPITAL BED THE FOLLOWING DAY, I HEARD DON'S booming voice creating chaos in the hallway. It was escalating with authority at someone. This was not my assertive "Let's have a conversation" husband. It was flat out aggression! He was making a lot of noise outside my room, making himself crystal clear to every nurse, doctor, and patient on the ward.

"Who's in charge here?" he yelled.

I heard a female respond but my mind didn't compute. Something awful was going down out there.

"What?" Don's voice got louder. "There's no way she's being released today! No way she's coming home!" His voice rose in aggravated tones with every expletive he spoke.

As I listened to the tension rise outside my room, I felt Jesus move near in the midst of the sounds.

I can't go home! my mind swirled. *I haven't even peed by myself! I haven't been out of this bed yet. Jesus, help Don!*

As I tried to focus on the doorway, I saw the same huge angel I'd seen before. This time he leaned his back against the wall near the door and waited. Jesus had sent this angel again, knowing he would step in and help Don protect me. I didn't see any wings, but the angel's massive presence took up the wall and doorway. I couldn't do a thing but wait in that bed, but I saw the liquid gold come and melt all over me. I was completely unafraid.

About an hour earlier, Don had received a call from the first MPI (Manitoba Public Insurance) adjuster assigned to my case. The adjuster informed Don that they were making arrangements to have me come home. I was being released, and Don was to come and get me immediately.

"I just came from HSC," Don informed him, totally rattled, "and there's no way she's coming home today." That was pretty much the end of their conversation, because the adjuster had just hit a brick wall smeared with foul expressions while talking to Don.

Although retired, Don was helping family at their pizza commissary at that time. He'd left work frantically and rushed back to the hospital. Once again, he was sweaty, but this time he smelled like pepperoni and pizza sauce. That's when I first heard him in the hall outside my door. "Who has been speaking with the MPI adjuster?" He bellowed at somebody.

Within minutes, Don realized that the nurses were totally unaware of my release.

He came around the curtained section looking upset and scared. He had that funny, tender look in his eyes that he gets when he doesn't know what to do for me. He walked right past the angel, completely unaware of the help God had sent. I think I smiled, knowing that the angel had done what he was sent to do—help Don.

As a former police officer, my Don had seen thousands of people in my condition, and he knew beyond a shadow of a doubt that I wasn't ready to go anywhere! He was also aware that the doctors still hadn't been able to thoroughly assess all my injuries. He noticed that both feet and legs were now casted up to my knees and resting on those soft pillows.

Don shook his head and angrily informed me that an MPI adjuster was suggesting that I be released straight from the trauma unit into the street. No way! Don believed that was the stupidest decision someone in upper management could make, especially without knowing all the facts. As my protector, his German shepherd-self surfaced—growling, snarling, and barking to keep me safe.

After several calls for clarification, I heard a nurse assure my upset, angry husband that his wife would not be going home anytime soon. They realized there had been an error and, unfortunately, inexperienced communication on MPI's part. Don calmed down and lovingly stroked his thumb over my hand. I saw the angel follow him out the door. I think I sighed.

After Don left, I recall that I was shaking and sweating but grateful for the angel who had come to watch over us. I was still barely able to lift or move my head. Again, the trusty little happy-oblivion needle was stuck into my awfully sore hip, and off to la-la land I went ... until the waking came again, and the crazy reality of pain crawled all over to consume the "me" that now lay in that bed. I was, however, consistently aware of the physical keeping of the Holy Spirit. He surrounded me completely with unfailing love, which spelled safety and peace and held me no matter what was happening.

Chapter

SIX

ONE DAY MORPHED INTO THE NEXT, BUT ABOUT TWO WEEKS AFTER I'D arrived at the HSC, I became more consistently aware of my surroundings. I didn't understand why or from where trays of food came. I wasn't sure what to do. I recall seeing bowls of pudding or soup moving around on the tray, and someone on staff would position the food so that I could try to aim it into my mouth. One time, someone gave me something to hold in my right hand. I looked at it and didn't know that it was called a spoon. I'm sure I looked confused, because the woman told me to use it to pick up the food. I aimed for one of the four spoons I saw floating back and forth. It looked to me like several bowls blurred together, but I stabbed at something. It didn't make any sense that stuff was not where it seemed to be. The tray of food confusion happened several times a day, every day.

Existing in that place didn't feel like anything. Nothing made sense, but I wasn't aware that nothing made sense. I was just there in that bed until one of the nurses asked, "Did you eat anything today?"

I felt confused and whispered, "I'm not sure."

"You have to try," she instructed gently.

Trying to eat became a task to master. I made a mess because my hands shook badly, so food never did find my mouth on the first try. Getting food from the tray into my mouth became a task I got better at. Chewing and swallowing hurt and fatigued me. Sucking water from a non-bend straw didn't work, as I couldn't bend over or sideways enough to take a sip by myself. It was exhausting. I had to wait for someone …

always waiting for someone to help me. Usually I didn't remember if someone had come or not.

There's a pretty common feeling among women that if you've had a baby, a certain degree of modesty gets chucked out the window. You feel pretty much overexposed to the immediate world around you. That was me for sure after the accident, because I couldn't bend to wash, stand to wash, or reach to wash any of my parts! I'd always taken care of my girly parts, and now others did that for me. I was too sick to care one whit! What a mess.

Every time I opened my eyes to wakefulness, I hurt somewhere. Moving my left hand and arm created a burning sensation on my left side. I didn't know then that broken ribs make people want to scream with every breath, cough, or sneeze. (My recommendation—don't do that! Screaming makes it move and hurt more.) I learned that my right arm movement called painful attention to the right shoulder area and down the back.

Help! Press a button with only the thumb and wait. Ahh! A nurse and a needle—oblivion! Wake up from the cave hearing voices. Sheer exhaustion.

I didn't think beyond the moment or remember what or who had done or said what or when. I breathed. Breathed high up. Never low into the lungs. Too painful. Shallow breathing. Then awareness came to one area of my mind: *I can't see stuff. I'm looking, but I only see blurry stuff that moves all over. Aha! I wear glasses. Where are they? Sheesh! No wonder I can't see!* I was becoming conscious of my internal dialogue.

At some point I heard a tap, tap, tap, and then a woman with a name tag marched into the curtained-off area. "Hi. I'm your occupational therapist—OT, for short. I heard there's been a misunderstanding."

She stood at the end of the bed. Pretty lady with confident eyes. "You're sure not going home just yet," she stated. "I heard someone told you that you were going home. Well, not today, not just yet."

Relief. "I don't think I can," I breathed, tears streaming down my cheeks.

"Someday," she assured me. "But not until I okay it all." She smiled. "Nobody can release you—not MPI, not even the ortho doctors—I have the final say. You're not ready yet."

* * *

I must have drifted off, because I don't remember her leaving. I remember faces of friends and family. I heard their voices, but I couldn't tell if they were coming to visit or leaving.

Toward the end of the second week, a man stood on one side of my bed and said, "Hi. I'm a physiotherapist from rehab. They called me to come assess you."

Strong. He looked strong and smiled as he asked, "Have you been up yet?"

"Nope," I squeaked.

"Let's see how it goes." He continued to move around cheerfully.

I felt the bed motor hum, raising my top half into a sitting position. My head started to shake. Nausea rolled in, and I struggled to keep my eyes open. We waited as the room swam, spun, and swayed. I panted, taking little puffs of air and blowing out slowly. He wrote on his chart for a while.

"We can try another day," he offered.

"No, please," I begged, not knowing any better. "Let me try. Help me try. Jesus will help me try."

Skeptical but willing, he nodded. "Okay, let's see what you can do. Let's try to get your legs over this side of the bed so you can face me."

I tried to focus on him. To me he looked like a moving target.

"Just let me move your one leg a bit at a time," he encouraged, "and you adjust using your bum muscles."

Okay. Little by little I got to sit sideways and noticed white-casted legs dangling, pulling on my body. My hands and arms wouldn't support me. I couldn't stay upright, so I pitched forward onto him. Oh man! I was beginning to slide down. My body wasn't listening to my thoughts!

"Nurse!" yelled the strong physio guy. "I need some help here! Now!"

Struggling to hold me, he said, "Let's get you back in bed. You're not at all ready."

Two nurses came running.

"Please," I stupidly begged, sucking air a little at a time in gasps, with my face planted into this man's chest. Not having a clue as to what my body could and could not do, I pleaded, "Let me try. Just try. I can do it! Help me."

Well, picture this—one nurse on the left and one on the right. The big old physio boy bracing himself and propping me up on himself in front of my dangling casted legs, which were nearly on the floor.

"Where can we touch you?" I heard from one of them. I'm not sure what I told them.

"She's not supposed to weight bear, you guys," stated one nurse.

"Really? (Nasty expletive!) Oops! O brother!"

By now I had pitched forward into the man I trusted to help me. I felt my face planted somewhere on his body. I tried to stand as I continued to slip and slide off the bed.

"I can do this!" I insisted in my ignorance as I gritted through the ripping, biting pain. I was shocked that I couldn't. I was falling to the floor! I remember thinking, *They told me I wasn't going to die, so why can't I do this?*

I wish I'd fainted. I had three different people from three different angles trying to position themselves, with me moaning (more like screaming and crying), so as to get me back into that bed. If the impact hadn't killed me—this just might. However, now I was awake! I heard screeching. Must have been me!

Sweating like a pig, shaking, and doing all the other stuff pain makes people do kicked into high gear, but so did a pinprick of morphine!

"She's not ready," I heard the physio guy say as he faded away. "Who in their right mind called me to do this?"

"Not me," said the nurse. "Unbelievable!"

"Me neither!" said the second as all went dark.

Ahh! Blessed oblivion and the grey place.

* * *

After that first physio fiasco, I knew two things for sure: I wasn't going to die, and, somehow, I was going to get well … at home. The determined spirit in me revved up into the stubborn focus I'd had as a child. I believed if I stayed in that hospital, I'd fall into a hole and never come out. I determined that day to do whatever it took to get out of that bed and go home. Nobody could do it for me. I made up my mind. It was up to me.

"Jesus," I said, "show me how." There was no dialogue about how or when. He simply would.

Time became a blur as hospital staff came and went as the shifts changed. I was being taught skills my brain and body didn't remember. Meanwhile, I'd just talk to Jesus, sometimes in my prayer language the whole time, and sometimes in English. At times out loud, and other times not. I knew for sure that I was in His keeping here on earth and in that bed. In the ambulance, God had spoken out loud to me and breathed His breath into my ear: "Hedy, I will keep you." I believed God.

Teaching my brain to tell my body to sit up in the bed as the "up" button was pressed is still a nauseating memory that became an ongoing, never-ending nightmare to repeatedly live through. I had to relearn basic skills, because I was not going do die. Try getting on a bedpan in a bed after the catheter has been removed, with others holding you up so you don't fall sideways or forward. Heh! Way too much fun! And so it went—for hours and days.

But I didn't much care. Slowly a breath was easier. Each movement gained was more freedom. I began to realize that stubborn determination was good. I decided that I could and would pee without falling off that beggar of a bedpan … by myself and with that curtain shut! Small goal, you say? Don't knock it till you've done it. It's work getting well, and I was barely beginning to train for climbing my personal Mount Everest. Eventually the day came when, with the help of two nurses, I learned to manipulate my body off the bed and somehow relieve myself sitting on a commode just inches beside the bed. Those dear nurses looked away while holding on to me and standing guard on either side. New meaning for privacy for sure! Unfortunately, I also felt the awfulness of humiliation when I tried to make it on time, but my body failed.

Chapter

seven

"I cried out to the Lord, and he answered me from his holy mountain"
—Psalm 3:4

IT WAS A THURSDAY, TWO WEEKS AFTER THE MVA, WHEN I SAW THE purple bag with HSC stamped on it tucked into a corner on my hospital bed. I used a fork from my food tray to drag it over the sheets so I could look inside. My body began to tremble and shake. It was like looking at what was left of a person who had died. I realized it was what was left of what had been cut off my body. Clothes cut apart. The only "Real Bliss" jeans I'd ever owned. Cut open my "Olga" underpants and bra, and one runner minus the insert. Seeing my twisted eyeglasses, which Don had found at the crash site, with no lenses caused the tears to flow. The simple act of crying caused terrible physical pain, so it felt like even that act was cut off.

"Jesus," I addressed Him rather indignantly, "somebody cut off my clothes! Now they're wrecked!"

I also thought, *No wonder I can't see anything. I have no glasses on. Once I get glasses, maybe things won't spin so much.*

That was the day I realized how sick I was, but also from what I had been saved. I had almost died. It would have been easier for me if I had. The business of working to lift a spoon was exhausting. I lived in constant pain, continuous nausea, non-stop ringing, aching ears and aching eyes, constant gut cramping, a hurting chest and throat where tubes had been thrust in a hurry, and a rib cage that screamed, "Don't you breathe deep or sneeze! Ever!" My head felt like it was being tossed around like a dinghy in a storm.

My right arm and shoulder just hurt. It hurt to try and scratch any itch—anywhere, anytime!

The short of it is, if the patient can poop, pee, and pivot independently, chances for release get good—real fast. In the midst of this maze of activity, I knew I would live. I didn't know I would recover. I knew I was alive, and moment by moment I painfully breathed. Broken ribs are a pain.

Being present in a supernatural place of keeping is surreal. The Holy Spirit moves in tangible ways, much like conducting an orchestra. Each of the medical people played a part and were directed as needed by my Lord God. Since I am His and He is mine, why would this not be the case? That place of keeping is the most logical way of thinking and being; therefore, I lived moment by often agonizingly painful moment, seeing God orchestrate people in this system, whether they knew it or not. It didn't matter at all that I was totally incapable of helping myself to do much of anything except realize that I would recover at home not in hospital.

"Lord Jesus, please tell them to do things Your way for me," I asked.

He did. First, He placed a determined focus in me.

I desperately wanted to show the nurses I could "poop" on my own on a bedpan and not fall over. You see, after a big ol' whack to the head, stability and nausea become a constant challenge. Any movement—and I do mean any—caused unpleasant things to happen to my body. The walls swirled counter clockwise, the bed swayed, and the tiles on the floor swung back and forth, so focusing on a moving target (the bed pan) became all consuming.

Excruciating pain ripped everywhere, as breathing was a struggle. Suddenly, I would see eight nurses when in fact there were only two. It was weird to watch their faces, eyes, and hair get blurry as they moved. Fighting to keep my eyes open as fainting became the only pleasurable option was an added sensation. Involuntarily, my eyelids kept drooping shut. The physical need to urinate prevailed, because the other option was a diaper. Nada! Not me! Nope! Sucking in energy from outside myself assisted me on the steel pan.

The day finally came when I mastered the bedpan. It felt like a monumental victory. I had persevered and succeeded on my own, so I rejoiced loudly!

"I peed! I peed! Hey, I peed!" I squawked from my bed behind the curtain in a voice sounding very unlike the "me" before the accident. It was a voice that reflected the trauma of struggling for breath through incredible pain, a sound that emitted through a trachea that had hurriedly had all kinds of life supporting tubes shoved down it by emergency response people.

The momentous occasion was celebrated by nurses from "the desk," the orderly going by my door, and several resident doctors within earshot. Imagine, if you will, all these people rushing to where I was triumphant! Here they all were, standing at the end of my hospital bed and peering past the curtain at a woman perched on a bedpan, grinning and gasping and whose body and head were shaking uncontrollably from exertion. They were all laughing, cheering, and clapping. Somebody finally said, "Get her off there before she falls off."

Being cleaned up by caring nurses isn't so bad. I hadn't realized they did that! Hands moved me, cleaned me, and comforted me as joy expressed itself in silent weeping. Someone washed the sweat from my face. Somebody else brought a warmed thermal blanket. Slowly the shaking lessened. I slept, only to wake and find that I'd have to do it many times, again and again. Being successful in this endeavour became my top priority, and even in this my Lord had His angels assist, comfort, and minister encouragement by imparting a determination to get well. It started that day of my first successful attempt at independence regarding a most basic need. That determination grew as I became more familiar with that place deep inside called Courage, and the one true God who created that place in my heart.

* * *

Earlier I alluded to the hospital method I called "poop, pee, and pivot." I had accomplished Part One and Two of getting myself out of HSC and, in my mind, home. Now I made up my mind to focus on what it meant to "pivot."

From a physical therapist or OT perspective, the patient needs to be able (with assistance) to demonstrate the capacity to get upright into a sitting position on the bed and balance like that—repeatedly—with some measure of success. In a room that dances, swirls, and twirls around itself, it's similar to being the child who has just played "twirl and spin as long as you can" on the grass or swing and then taken the challenge of remaining upright. I trained myself to suck short breaths of air, focus with my eyes open, and stare at one target that I knew wasn't swaying. My brain registry scoffed, "Oh yes, it's moving!"

It was sheer determination beyond myself that propelled me to this next step. I had to allow my body to screech in pain, fight the constant nausea and dizziness, and learn to "bum walk" so my legs could dangle over the side of the bed. If I could do that in any given try without tipping over completely, I could see my next target: the commode. Getting to that formidable looking thing was what one nurse described as "the flusher brought to the patient. It will give you some independence," she assured me, "and help restore a bit of your dignity."

"Do what you gotta do" became synonymous with one goal, and that was to get muscles moving so I could go home. This challenge was more than my body could accomplish for days, and I only attempted the exertion after taking pain killers. I was pursuing two goals, so talk about exhaustion. Muscles are strange things. They have memory, and they most certainly let the brain know how they feel … again and again and again! Many times the song "I'll Fly Away" popped into my soul.

* * *

One morning after going through the whole rigmarole process of waking up, I saw the confident OT woman come into my room. I saw her lips move and I heard her voice, but I didn't understand the language she was speaking. Weird. She repeated herself, and after the third try, she looked at me and asked, "Can you hear me?"

"Yes," I squeaked, not daring to move my head.

"What did I say?" she insisted.

"Don't know," I responded. Puzzled, her face reflected concern.

By this time, I'd learned to gauge how well I was doing by the panic, concern, fear, or relief I saw in the doctors' and nurses' eyes. The OT then slowly spoke, deliberately pronouncing each syllable: "Have you been up and out of that bed yet?" This time I got it.

"No," I responded. Even chewing hurt, and thoughts kept slipping away into some hole.

Looking at her, I knew that was going to be the day I'd learn whether I would have a long hospital stay in the rehab centre or recover at home. The OT left saying, "I'll be back later." While she was gone, I made a decision. I would recover at home. That day I battled to gain more independence, despite incredible pain, nausea, dizziness, and fatigue. I would get to that commode at the edge of my bed to do all my personal business—with help or by myself.

Clearly the whack to my head had caused neurological issues. During the accident, my brain got sloshed around, causing all kinds of problems for me. This episode with the OT was the first of many interesting interactions! Early in my recovery, I'd give one-word answers in response to questions. I'd also watch a person's lips as they spoke, hoping I could figure out what was being said. Often I could hear their voice and see their lips moving, as well as their hand gestures and facial expressions, but I didn't know what was being said. I was listening, but it didn't log in.. As this intermittently continued, I got scared.

The reaction of family and friends was interesting, to say the least. Doctors and nurses got the "Oh my" look and repeated themselves in slow motion. We'd try again while they tried not to appear concerned as they made an obvious notation on their data chart. I underwent considerable neurological testing: how my eyes worked, how my ears connected to my brain, why the never-ending dizziness and nausea continued impeding my balance, and how delayed my mind had become. Medical professionals would say things like, "Well, you were bounced around quite a bit" or "It'll take time" or "How often does this happen?"

I, on the other hand, decided to engage with a long, laborious task of concentrating, listening, and hoping I'd "get it" so the poor soul in front of me wouldn't have to try again. I became more and more mentally fatigued. When the blank-out pause happened, friends and family were just so glad I was alive, they'd retry to communicate again … for years. Some patiently, others not so much.

In response, I worked hard to recover. Often a reply for me was like looking at the mail slot on the wall of an old rural post office. There should have been lots of words there ready to be used. There were times it was like looking at empty slots—no words ready for use. There used to be lots of words there, and I used them at will. Other times, a word here or there would appear, and sometimes I got wrong words, scrambled words, or confusing phrases. I had a lot of awkward pauses in my speech.

These issues were certainly disconcerting, but only when I was actually aware of them. One sure clue that I was struggling was the look on the individual's face. Duh! What did she just say? Ummmm. They'd look to whoever was with me for help: Don, Andrea, Aaron, or Wilma, questioning, "What *did* she mean? What did she just say?"

Sometimes they knew, other times not. Sometimes I was aware, sometimes not.

Months later when this dialogue happened in a group setting, I'd know I'd said something odd when the conversation came to a standstill and the eyes glazed over or the gazes filled with uncertainty or pity. The best, though, was when someone tried not to laugh!

Once during a family dinner, I *thought* I'd said I wanted to get myself more turkey. What I told them, blissfully unaware, was that I needed to scratch my ear! I heard them burst with laughter, and one of them said something to the effect that they hoped my "ear" tasted good!

Another hilarious conversation took place with Andrea. We were talking about packed- away toys, and I asked her about her red "darbie ball." I thought she'd fall off the couch, she laughed so hard. By now I was laughing as I asked, "What *did* I say?"

Barely able to contain herself, she managed, "You meant Barbie doll, Mom. Barbie doll!"

One day Don saw me rummaging through my purse, looking for my "starking picker." He came to help me and asked what I was looking for. I insisted I needed my "starking picker." He clued in and pulled out my handicapped parking sticker!

"Looking for this?" he laughed. We both did! Starking picker! Phooy!

On and on it went. Sometimes I got so tired of the endless fatiguing feeling that accompanied simply being upright.

* * *

Dogged determination is a good thing when it's helpful and not destructive. Some refer to it as stubborn behaviour, but I call it reaching deep inside for courage and using all the provision the Spirit has imparted to work at getting well. At that place and time, I knew I would survive the horrible accident. Something I couldn't even define propelled me.

One day during the third week of my lying in that hospital bed, a young man (kinda cute, too) introduced himself as the physiotherapy department head. Immediately I asked him, "Are you going to help me get out of here? I want to get better at home."

His eyes flickered slightly. "Yes, and we'll start today."

"Now?" I pleaded.

He proceeded to assess my abilities and injuries and said, "Not yet. Not today. Oh, by the way, how many faces do I have?"

"Ummm ... one?" I guessed as he turned to leave. "Please," I begged, "let me try. Help me try."

He turned around, grinned a bit, and the process began. I had to move if I was ever going anywhere. Well, all I can say is I tried, and my body didn't work. Couldn't make it past the legs dangling over the side of the bed. The room tilted and rocked. The young man buzzed, yelling, "I need help here!"

I had tried to stand up on my own. That was my goal. I was shocked that I couldn't. My body would not obey my brain! That poor soul knew getting me back into bed would require several people, and it did. Painfully. I remember thinking, *I need to learn to pivot, and then they'll let me go home.*

Once I was back in bed, he patted my hand and said, "Good try, but it'll be a while yet."

I cried in defeat. Physical, emotional, and spiritual pain hurts. It just plain old hurts. I cried ... carefully ... because crying with broken ribs and a gut injury is nasty! Real nasty. Someone gave me a shot, and I disappeared into the grey place of unconsciousness or induced sleep.

* * *

"Answer me when I call, O God of my righteousness! You have given me relief when I was in distress. Be gracious to me and hear my prayer!"
—Psalm 4:1, ESV

During these painful weeks in the hospital, Jesus was present in a tangible, unquestionable way. He and I conversed all the time. I talked and He helped me, encouraged me, and kept me with every breath I took. Later I heard that staff and patients on the ward knew about the "lady who prays all the time." At the time, I thought the various members of the hospital staff took good care of their patients by being attentive. Staff often poked their noses around the corner of the door, or through the flapping curtain. Sometimes they stood quietly and looked at me thoughtfully, or took a moment to say hi. Some smiled and said, "I hear you're a miracle." The doubting ones would ask, "Does God really talk to you?"

What else could I say but "Yup," suck in a breath, "and He'll talk to you too, if you want."

As you can imagine, the responses varied, but that's God's business, not mine. I wasn't capable of taking care of anybody. I knew my caring Lord could, would, and did.

Apparently, the presence of Jesus was so evident in my room, people in the hall often stopped and stared. Some knew His presence, some didn't, but all were affected. Often I'd wake up and hear myself praying audibly in my prayer language. I knew God was God, and I was His—forever.

Simple tasks, like holding a soup spoon and aiming it successfully all the way from a bowl to my mouth, became a necessary goal. Sometimes it was funny trying to decide which of the four moving objects was the real soup spoon. Other times it was easier just to find a straw and suck. If someone was nearby, they'd help me, or I'd say, "Just forget it."

I'd hear my Lord from within say, "Eat of Me; I'll sustain you," or "Come, child." I didn't participate in any part of life without consciously knowing Jesus's presence.

Although true, that verse was not in my thoughts as I breathed life in moment by moment, concentrating only on, "If I breathe too deep, I'll hurt. If I involuntarily twitch even in my sleep, I'll wake up moaning, because everything from my hair follicles to my toenail hurts."

But from within, God's peace would come. A soothing rehabilitation, like a soft baby blanket wrapped around me while I spasmed and hurt.

"The angel of the Lord encamps around those who fear him, and rescues them"

—Psalm 34:7, NASB

Chapter
eight

AMONG THE HOSPITAL STAFF THAT CAME AND WENT WAS AN ORDERLY. I'd noticed him before, pushing patients around in a wheelchair. He'd even been in to take my roommate for a "ride" to somewhere I had not yet been. I'd only gotten out on a rolling bed for MRIs, X-rays, and CT scans. Usually everyone came my way to assess progress.

One day after the second physio attempt, I saw that orderly in the hallway at my door. He poked his head around the corner. I finger waved and smiled.

"You been up yet?" he asked, grinning.

"Ummm … a bit, I think. Not really sure." I rasped in my strange, squeaky thin voice.

He smiled, redirected his wheelchair, and left.

Silently, I called … *please wait for me.*

Later that day, he came back and asked again. "You been up yet?" He grinned again and left.

This time I suddenly came out of my personal head fog. It dawned on me as I realized, *This guy is my ticket out of here! Jesus, you sent me help. He's my Part Three. Pivot!*

That's when I decided to practise. I practised when nobody was there to caution or watch me tilt, topple, or slump. I figured I couldn't get better just lying there. Nobody could get well for me. I practised moving my arm until it obeyed me and located the button to slowly, inch by inch, move my upper body into a sitting position. I'd wait and push through the pain and sloshing nausea, trying not to barf so that no one would come running. I'd ever so slowly lower myself back down—shaking, covered in sweat, and longing for the grey place of nothingness.

I don't remember how many times a day I tried this, or for how long I could stay upright. Eventually, I could manage for a bit. Huge progress, I figured. Day after day I'd ask a doctor or nurse if I could go home yet. They'd smile and say things like, "Not yet" or "Let's see" or "Give yourself time."

The best one was a nurse who exclaimed, "Oh my dear, you've *got* to be *kidding!*"

Well, I wasn't. Not much of the old me was working, but I knew I had a ticket out.

Days merged as many dear, sweet faces of caring, supportive, and praying family and friends came and went. I know I kept telling them I saw them in Jesus, and how Jesus was really one with the Father. I'd seen that God the Father, God the Son, and God the Holy Spirit are truly one. I knew this to be truth with every sucking breath! They are one not only in Heaven but here on this earth. I am still in complete awe and wonder at this truth today.

I continued to practise alone with my bed button when no one was around. Mr. Orderly, as I named him, continued to poke his head around the corner. I'd smile, because I knew what he'd say: "You been up yet?"

Toward the end of my third week in the trauma unit, I surprised him with a "yup." The truth was, I'd I managed to get to the commode with the assistance of two nurses on either side propping me up so I wouldn't fall off the thing. I figured that was good enough!

After a while he came back with a wheelchair. Freedom! He pushed that dreadful commode away and whipped his chair into position. He waited for me to push my button and slowly get into a sitting position. My eyes never left his face. He instructed me to turn toward him. I thought about that, and as I did, my body moved (by itself, it seemed). Before I could catch my breath, he had his hands and arms in position to lift and lower me into a softly- cushioned wheelchair.

He laughed as he rolled me into the hallway. "Don't you dare fall out! Keep your head straight and those eyes open."

Slowly, I emerged out of that cocoon of a room and into the world. I heard clapping and encouraging voices:

"You go, girl!"

"Way to go, Hedy!"

"What are you doing out of bed?"

Suddenly, my ride stopped and in front of me, hunkered down on his haunches, was one of two doctors I remembered from Step Down. Dr. B.'s eyes looked at me at eye level, and he asked, "How'd you get in there?" Rapping the wheelchair with his hand, he glanced up at Mr. Orderly.

"Jesus helped me," I rasp-squeaked. "I asked Him to help you when you didn't know what to do with me."

He spoke thoughtfully. "I wondered what happened when we didn't have to go in."

I knew Dr. B. meant cut me open to check out what they call the black hole, which occurs when severe trauma to a gut presents with swelling that makes someone look six months pregnant.

Between gasps of breath, I told him, "I asked Jesus to help you not make a mistake you'd have to live with. I saw you in a holy huddle talking with others. You said, 'Wait, wait you guys.'"

Surprised, he took my trembling hand. "That's true. That's what happened, and you did what we always hope for. You threw up."

"That was all the orange stuff I saw!" I smiled.

He chuckled, stood, and told somebody to get me back to bed.

"Thank you for helping, Jesus," I whispered as I felt the wheelchair move.

Then I heard Dr. B. call, "Wait!"

Next thing I knew, he and another doctor were kneeling on either side of that wheelchair in the hall. "We're on our way to the OR to open up a black hole now. We have to do this one. Will you please pray for us?"

Somehow, Jesus lifted both my arms up and put my hands on their bowed heads. I prayed out loud, stating that Jesus would help them. They left and I heard someone say, "Well, that's a first."

Mr. Orderly whispered in my ear, "Well, Mrs. Wiebe, you've had quite the first day out! Now let's figure out how to get you back in bed."

Sweating, shaking, nauseated, everything rolling around counter clockwise, and exhausted … I was ready to go back.

Chapter

nine

DURING THE FOURTH WEEK OF AUGUST, 1999, I SET OUT TO CONVINCE any staff who would listen that I was ready to go home. Leaving the hospital after being in a highway traffic accident that caused multiple serious injuries is quite the process. The mega-institutional system of the Manitoba Public Insurance gets involved in the life of an accident victim, especially if one was a passenger. Wading through the process are the doctors I call the "legs guy," the "gut guy," the "head guy," and the chief resident of the trauma team (called the Gold Service Team). Add to this the hospital physiotherapist from the rehab, the occupational therapist, the social service assistance people, and the homecare people. Yikes! All of their reports have to co-ordinate before a projected release date is discussed.

I waited, worked hard to do the Three Ps, and repeatedly stated that I knew I could get well better and faster at home from my own bed. I persistently pushed to go home. Finally, toward the end of the fourth week of August, the morning came to leave. I was propped up in a wheelchair in a hospital stretcher transport van.

By the time I got home, the "mobility guy," the OT, and the handicap van transportation guy were there, as were Don and Andrea. Each person seemed to have a function. The mobility guy and the OT were figuring out what I needed in order to stay at home. The transportation guy and Don were figuring out how to get me out of the van, up the front door steps in the wheelchair, and into the house without hurting me too badly. Someone decided ramps would be needed, as well as a smaller wheelchair, because the one I was in was way too big.

Home. Drugged up, but home. I was elated.

* * *

Once home, the task of getting into our queen-sized bed became a nightmare to me. Poor Don and Andrea were distressed seeing me so sick, and the OT had to decide if I could remain at home or if I needed to go back and be admitted into the rehabilitation hospital at HSC.

"Lord, please, I don't want to go back," I called. I begged the OT to let me stay.

Jesus heard. He enabled my take-action, be-motivated, get-things-done husband of many years. In just over four hours, he had dismantled our bed, gone with the mobility guy to his shop, moved a broken-down hospital bed into his truck, and driven out of town to a friend in Starbuck, Manitoba, who could fix anything! This friend of Don's showed love with his actions and went about setting up a highly functional single hospital bed. Don brought it back and set it up in our bedroom by himself.

I don't have a clue where I was propped up in the house or who all was there. I remember the fabulously beautiful face of my Andrea, and I knew I was in awful pain but too scared to say a word, in case the OT insisted I go back with her to the hospital. I was glad I didn't see Aaron's face, because his logically-minded swing vote would have agreed with the OT that I go back to the hospital. I was determined to recover at home with lots of help. In retrospect, it would have been easier on all of us had I let myself be transferred to recovery for a few months at the Sherbrook Rehabilitation Centre right next to HSC. At the time, however, I felt immense gratitude once in that bed.

Days later we recognized more loss. Don and I couldn't hold each other in that hospital bed. He felt the separation much more keenly than I. I couldn't take care of anyone or anything. I couldn't even take care of myself. Others did that. Don had moved our queen-sized mattress into our basement. It was a terrible time for him. He cried alone downstairs; I cried alone upstairs. Sometimes he'd hold me where I could be held without pain, and we'd cry together.

Don could run away from his feelings. He had two legs and a body that let him get busy and work, like the way we take flight or fight when we're scared. Don took flight. He escaped that house and me every chance he got. He became obsessively busy helping our brother-in-law at one of his businesses, Gondola Enterprises, a commissary where all the food for the restaurants gets processed. Don buried himself there. During the fall of 1999, I rarely saw him during the week. He'd come home exhausted from "running" and would eat supper with his face buried in his plate. He'd come to our bedroom to say goodnight after I'd gotten settled. Sometimes he'd still stink like old pizza sauce because he hadn't bothered to shower. This wonderful, generous-hearted man struggled to stay afloat. He knew he was helpless to make me well.

At night, all alone, I would often become sad, especially because I couldn't be with Don in the same bed. Any movement sent shooting pain somewhere in my body. Sometimes I'd ask Jesus if He'd send the angel to watch over Don and help him to not feel as alone. I'd cry on the inside and be sad without moving, because sobs created a domino effect in muscles, and that hurt more.

Alone in my room, which was next to Andrea's bedroom, I could hear her breathe, talk to herself, and sing or cry at night. She had been forced into a task that was way over her head. I didn't want her to be the primary caregiver, but for a while she was. Remarkably, she was the one who knew exactly what to do to help. It was way too big an ask of a seventeen-year-old. The load was too heavy for her to carry.

Alone, I'd hear Aaron come home from being out with his lovely fiancée, Wilma, as they planned their wedding and dreamed of their future. I'd wonder who this woman was he called his mother. He'd quietly walk past my bedroom door and pause and listen. If I let him know I was awake, he'd come in and talk awhile. That was rehab too. I still got to be his mom, but it was all different. He didn't know what his mom would be like in two months, a year, or more. I was incapable of being anything he might have needed his mom to be.

Because of one woman's careless mistake, both Aaron and Andrea lost the vibrant mom they had known. The woman they knew and loved was gone. There I was—alive but completely different. A physically pitiful mess.

Don had lost his first love. She had disappeared in the blink of an eye, and now he was alone—but not really, because this other woman in our bedroom was alive.

We were all in this deep trauma, but to varying degrees. Often we were recovering well one day and swirling miserably the next. Oh, but God. Yes … oh, but God. He had sent His angels again and again to bring courage to us all, just like He promised. Some of us saw them or felt them.

We began to live in a new normal.

1 Thessalonians 5:23-24 reads:

Now may the God of peace make you holy in every way, and may your whole spirit and soul and body be kept blameless until our Lord Jesus Christ comes again. God will make this happen, for he who calls you is faithful.

I realized I hadn't gotten to stay in heaven, and Jesus had not yet come back, so I'd better learn to live on earth His way.

For the first months at home, my conscious awareness of myself consisted of what I call "things of the Spirit to spirit." My mind and body functioned poorly, but I knew that my God held me all the time. His faithfulness called to me when my eyes opened and the painful awareness of my body surfaced within seconds. It felt like every cell known to man hurt. It was getting old real fast! Often God's physical presence as *courage* descended as my eyes blinked or my head twitched and waves of nausea and constant dizziness enveloped me like the rolling tide. Then the sense of falling backwards into an endless place would begin, and His stillness would enter while I waited for the sickening nausea and sloshing to lessen so I could make it onto the ever-present bedpan or commode a caregiver shoved under me. (Personally, I think the bedpan and commode at the hospital had little scurrying legs that followed me home! They couldn't simply let me be—the little beasts!)

Eventually, I would make it to the commode beside my bed after a process of sheer determination, much like a climber pursuing the top of a mountain without falling. One determined step became one move after the other. Then victory and the long road down the mountain. It was an arduous task of making it to my "water closet" and getting back to the bed, only to begin the painful task of lying down. Each movement required more strength than I had. Many times, strength or determination weren't enough. But, because the Holy Spirit indwelled me, He was faithful. I was often gratefully aware only of Him as I blissfully fell unconscious in sleep. I was learning this lesson—perseverance and plain old stubbornness would help me master many other ways to live a new way.

Oh, I heard people sounds, but that's all they were—sounds, touches, prodding—but the "being alive" was in the Spirit. My senses had become more sensitive, and I heard God speaking to me all the time. A faithful, tangible, loving Keeper spoke so that I could live one moment to the next, often blissfully unaware of anything but my Lord God.

"*What I whisper in your ears, shout from the housetops for all to hear!*" (Matthew 10:27b). Many were the "whisperings" during the hours that turned into days and then stretched into weeks, months, and years. Some things I remember seemed more profound than others, but all invited me to "*Taste and see that the Lord is good*" (Psalm 34:8a). Other times I begged for mercy to run away from myself, just like King David talked about in the book of Psalms.

I was being introduced to God's ways, which are good. All good. In every way good. All-the-time good. Did it always feel good in the physical parts of my being? Nope! Absolutely not!

Chapter ten

REHABILITATION OF MY BODY BEGAN SLOWLY. THE WHACK TO MY HEAD left me seeing double, triple, or quadruple, but I learned to trust that there was only one. I also got good at navigating on what felt like moving ground. I'd laugh and say, "Lord, I gave up my drinking days on purpose! Now I get a free drunk—all day, every day!"

I'd hoped that getting new glasses would help with my vision problems. Boy, was I in for a surprise! The world I now lived in spun and moved whenever I moved my head, swallowed, or blinked. Nope, all the new glasses did was let me see clearly that objects and people who had been a blur before were clearly four faces of the same person, or four pictures in a row when only one hung on the wall. I could now see distinctly enough to know approximately where to put my hand so I could hold a spoon. A cup full of liquid was often way too much work to get off the tray to my lips and back. The effort made me sweat, and for the first time in my life, I couldn't have cared less whether I ate or drank.

Having both ankles casted up to my knees, with no-weight-bearing order, meant that I needed to learn to navigate everything from a wheelchair. My arms weren't strong enough to hold the weight of my Bible, and my eyes refused to focus on the letters. Eventually I learned to feed myself, but it was months before I could do my own hair or get dressed on my own.

My ears couldn't tolerate most sounds. I didn't know at the time that because of the tubes thrust down my throat, it would be a long time before I could sing again. All I knew was that my chest was black, green, and blue and hurt like heck! But I could sing in the Spirit in my prayer language even as the broken ribs healed.

The severe trauma to the gut often produced ripping, scary spasms to the point where one day Don and Andrea called 911 to take me back to HSC. Moaning, crying, and writhing, I begged the paramedics to let me stay home, because I somehow knew that if I went back to the hospital, I'd have to stay there a long time. I'd been given several morphine tablets to take home in case the pain got too bad. Somebody gave me one, and eventually the ambulance guys and my family decided to listen to my distress and not send me back. I went into the grey place again.

During that time, I lived in a "holy bubble." God's faithfulness called, His courage descended, and His stillness entered, creating a singular focus of sheer determination that I would get well … weller-er-er-er. Not surprisingly, prayer became synonymous with my body's need for oxygen or water. I would die without them, and I would spiritually die without the ongoing communication with my Lord.

For the first few weeks at home, the days began pretty much the same way. My eyes would open and I'd wait until the room stopped rolling around. When the sensation of falling backwards into nothingness minimized, I'd ask for help (usually from Andrea or Don) to the commode. With non-weight-bearing legs, I needed help back to bed. Then I'd wait until the shaking and trembling slowed down and I could lie still.

The doorbell would ring at 8:00 a.m., and someone would call out, "Homecare." I'd hear footsteps and soon see a new person at my bed, telling me their name. Their faces reflected all sorts of things as they asked how they could help me. Usually I didn't know. I simply thanked them for coming. Repeat and repeat. Most didn't know what to do for someone in my condition. Sometimes the OT would come, assess, and tell me I was doing great but wasn't ready for physio or any kind of rehabilitation. Then they would set up a bunch of appointments and leave.

* * *

One morning rehabilitation started abruptly when our doorbell rang at 8:00 a.m. Courage came to me. The penetrating, incessant ringing of our doorbell sent our dog, Dudley, from a low growl right into a frenzy of loud barking (like German shepherd in a small watchdog—*loud*). Struggling,

I fought to wake up, realizing that this new homecare worker hadn't been given instructions to come to the front door and simply knock, say hello, and come in. Severe trauma to the gut plus broken ribs affected my ability to take a breath deep enough to yell, "Come in."

The doorbell continued to ring, and the dog's barks escalated. Slowly, something registered within me. *It's the back doorbell!* I was alone in the house. Everyone was out: Don at the commissary, Andrea at her new job selling Clinique at a large department store, and Aaron at theology classes at Providence University College. If I didn't get that door, the caregiver would leave and I'd be on my own all day! I'd barely learned to master the ordeal that got me to the commode beside my bed. I knew that I couldn't take care of myself. I heard myself crying and begging in tongues for help.

Familiar burning, searing pain made itself known as I emerged from a drug-induced sleep. I tried to roll over, sit up, and bum walk so I could hang my heavily-casted legs over the side of the bed without pitching forward— flat on my face!

The wheelchair wasn't within reach, but my trusty "grabber" was. Hooking onto the arm of the chair, I pulled. It felt like pulling a stuck rock. The ever-present nausea produced bile, the head made me unstable, the legs didn't work, and the rest of me silently screamed in pain. Still the doorbell rang nonstop, and Dudley was barking like crazy by now. My ears hurt. I desperately wanted it all to *stop*.

Once again, my prayer language arose within and a determination beset me. A determination so powerful rose up that adrenalin shot to new heights, and somehow my body swung itself into that chair. Imagine Jesus to the rescue in real time!

Talk about singular focus. I grabbed the wheelchair wheels to roll forward, but I couldn't move myself! Looking down, I thought, *I'm on carpet.* Wheelchairs and carpet don't dance. I had no upper body power. Using my casted heels to propel myself forward and my hands to inch the wheels forward, the marathon ride from the bedroom down the hall to the kitchen began. Eventually I hit kitchen linoleum! On I went toward the back door, where Dudley's barking, continuous ringing, and loud knocking seemed deafening to me. If I could have shot that doorbell, I believe I would have.

The back door was two steps down, and I was higher up. I attempted to whack the inside door with the backdoor broom. The caregiver heard something, and the ringing thankfully stopped long enough for me to pant, "Come in!"

"The door is locked!" she shouted irritably.

I focused on the blurry doorknob. I saw four of them and aimed for one. By now my body was beginning to shake from exhaustion, and I figured I better pop that doorknob to unlock it. Once again, the broom became my hands and arms. It gripped the knob and as I twisted, the door came unlocked. The annoying sounds from outside ceased and in stumbled a woman. Even Dudley was quiet.

She was a homecare lady unlike any I'd ever seen. She appeared as dishevelled and grumpy on the outside as she must have been on the inside. A deep growl rumbled in Dudley's chest as he stood his ground to protect me. Her face registered shock then whipped into fear as she looked at me and my trusty four-footed warrior.

Swearing, she declared, "I'm not coming in with that dog here!"

Dudley growled long and low as he sensed that it was not the wind of the Holy Spirit who had blown into his house!

Beginning to pitch sideways and forward, I begged, "Just help me to bed. Please push me. Just help me, please!"

By now my body was in serious trouble and the dizziness had reached dangerous heights.

As she rolled her eyes she snorted, "Nobody told me about all this! Nobody told me I'd have somebody like you!" Along with this, she spewed out a string of expletives.

That day introduced me to a world that gives new meaning to the word *survivor*! I wished I could pass into that blissful, unconscious place, because in addition to physical pain, the anguish of thinking began in earnest.

Jerkily she shoved the wheelchair around, crashing my casted feet into the kitchen table. I know I screamed. I felt cornered and couldn't get away from her. I begged Jesus to give her a new language. Her English was awful!

Again, I heard her, "Oh no! I'm so sorry. I've never pushed one of these things before!" The profanity continued. Her language was worse than what comes out of a sewer hole!

I felt us banging into every door we passed through the hall. It was like an endless nightmare of fear and pain I couldn't escape from. All I heard was her profanity.

Finally, I saw my bed. There was no way I wanted that woman to touch me. Somehow, I grabbed her arm, and I believe God supernaturally swung me around and out of the wheelchair, because I was gently lifted onto the bed. I slowly and carefully lowered my head and body down, grabbed the plastic bucket nearby, and barfed.

Again I heard nasty expletives, "Oh brother! What a mess!"

By now I couldn't function. I lay there begging, "Lord, you said you would keep me! You promised! Make her shut up!"

She was so inept, it was hard to believe. She didn't know how to care for me. She constantly swore and asked stupid questions:

"How am I supposed to clean up this mess?"

"I don't know how to do this!"

"How am I supposed to feed her?"

"Do you want toast?"

"Can you make yourself some eggs or something?"

"Do you like coffee?"

"Where do you keep your coffee?"

"How do you make coffee?"

On and on she went. Finally, after I'd told her three times where the cutlery drawer was, I lost it! I told her to be quiet, leave the bedroom, and close the bedroom door.

After a while she knocked, told me she had made me toast, and set it beside the bed with a glass of fresh water. Inwardly I cringed, wanting her to leave, but she didn't. Instead, she stared and said, "Your face is glowing."

I tried to grin. "That's Jesus."

She stomped to the end of my bed, hand on her hips, and mockingly commented, "And I'll bet you see angels too."

"Yes," I answered, still sweating, shivering, and shaking.

"Yeah, well so do I!" she exclaimed loudly. She took a deep breath and began to unload the many episodes that she believed to be angelic encounters. She waved her arms willy-nilly around her head as her eyes frantically darted back and forth.

"I see them everywhere too! They're going crazy!" she exclaimed.

A brief deep guttural tone escaped from her throat, and the hair on my neck stood up. Now when that happens to me, it's not a good thing. Evil is surely present. I felt like my body was pasted into my bedsheets, so I faked falling asleep and once again prayed in tongues. (I couldn't' think fast enough to pray in English!) I begged for the love of Jesus to light the darkness that had entered my room and make it go away. She noisily left the room, slamming the door.

Suddenly, I smelled cigarette smoke. It made me gag. Coughing with broken ribs was not a party I wanted to be at! I realized she was smoking in the house! I rang the little bell beside the cold toast on the night table, and eventually she poked her head around the corner. By now I was mad, and as loudly as possible I croaked, "Put out your smoke, and in Jesus's name, get out of my house! Get out! Just get out now!"

She yelled back, "You'll be all alone! Don't you dare get me fired!"

I heard her swear yet again, slam the back door, and leave. It was the longest day. Ever.

Hearing Andrea come home later brought on hysterical sobbing and tears of relief. Poor Andrea! She assessed the situation and sat down beside a woman who trembled, shook, and certainly didn't resemble the mother she'd always known. I cried while she gently cleaned up the smelly mess of the day, which included all of me.

After Don found out about my day … well, I'm thankful that foul-mouthed woman wasn't in our house. He would have "escorted" her out on her tippy-toes! He was madder than I had been!

That was the day I learned an important lesson and spiritual truth. The devil loves chaos! My God helps the helpless and does serious business with sin, but He loves that sinner just as much as He loves me.

Angels are God's messengers who do His bidding and His bidding alone. We are not to believe *in* them. We are to believe in the one who *sends* them. That's why the devil likes to disguise his miserable old self as an angel of light to those who don't know better.

God has told us:

Don't let anyone capture with empty philosophies and high-sounding nonsense that come from human thinking and from the spiritual powers of this world, rather than from Christ. For in Christ lives all the fullness of God in a human body. So you also are complete through your union with Christ, who is the head over every ruler and authority.
—Colossians 2:8–10

Every angel I've ever seen reflected Jesus to me, pointed me to God's powerful love as demonstrated in the finished work of Jesus on the cross for the forgiveness of all sin, and produced in me reverential awe of my Almighty God, whose great power is much bigger than anything Satan dreams up!

No wonder the evil one nips at someone's Achilles heel when they are down, or tries to "devour a victim" at their worst. My body had become a victim of a motor vehicle accident that changed my life as I knew it, but … the real, alive me was *not* a *victim*. I was not a victim in my spirit and would not become one in my mind.

The devil can only "devour" someone who is a victim and stays a victim. I remember asking Jesus to show Himself to the homecare woman so that the deceit she'd worn like a huge ill-fitting trench coat would blow off her. I asked Him to get her a new coat.

Together the Wiebe family made a decision that day. No one in our family, especially not our beautiful eighteen-year-old daughter, should need to be a steady primary caregiver for me. It was way too hard on us. Somehow we would get homecare, and someone other than family would consistently care for me during the day. As a family, we asked our Lord Jesus to send help and direct homecare to hear our request. We also asked for a helpful assistant from the Manitoba Public Insurance.

The next morning, I awoke to the sound of a quick knock. I heard the front door open and a friendly, singsong voice say, "Good morning. Homecare."

I heard steps. Dudley didn't even have time to rouse his little ol' self and bark. I looked up and there stood a tall, dark-haired young woman with hands on her hips.

"Well, honey, you look like somebody needs to take care of you."

She shook her head side to side and smiled as she said, "I'm Liz."

All I could breathe was, "Tag. You're it."

Thus began eight months of knowing a wonder of God's creation in the form of one loving, caring, no-nonsense woman. God sent Liz to help me, and I knew it. She cooked, washed, and cleaned up after me. She showed me that if she held my right arm just so, I could comb my own hair ... sort of. She treated me with dignity as she taught me how to have a shower with rubber-like, full-length leg hoses carefully manoeuvred over my casts and synched at my thighs. I could then slide onto a seat *and* not fall off the sturdy bench stuck somewhere on the bathtub! She did laundry and emptied that blasted ever-present commode, all without ever once making me feel like I was a burden.

God can use anybody He wants to when a child of His needs help! I never heard her swear, not once! I loved that lady. As a family, we appreciated her no-nonsense approach and learned to appreciate every part of what she offered. Frankly, I don't know what we'd have done without her. God sent her. I'm as sure as the nose on my face that He gave Liz a memo and told her to come to our house.

I also began to learn that my thinking was a bit scrambled. Often, I was like a happy jack rabbit, with thoughts hopping, skittering, and leaping in seemingly no direction at all. Thoughts could be in pursuit of something, but then they'd get lost. Gone ... someplace. Thoughts banged around in my head, repeatedly not going anywhere. It felt as futile as trying to catch the tail of that jack rabbit. I'd tell my Lord Jesus that I needed a way to trap these "every which way direction" thoughts, to snare one and keep it. Yes, I wanted catch just one and see what might be there.

Chapter
eleven

Trauma leaves devastation in its wake, and it comes in many ways. Anyone who has experienced an event or series of events that smashed into their life will know that life, or a part of it, stopped as they knew it on that day. The loss is devastating. What had been devastated? What had broken in my life?

Walking at will was huge. Being able to see only one of everything like I used to. Hopping in my car to get groceries, or taking off for the beach with a friend. Taking a deep breath to sing songs in musicals or a church choir. Competing in a music festival with other voices in my range, leading a children's choir, singing in the worship band with a bunch a of energetic young people, or performing at weddings and funerals. To once more run, ride my bike down the trail at the river, skip, twirl around in dance, dial a phone successfully and track the numbers in sequence, speak without stuttering, or simply make my own cup of coffee! Mostly, I missed being able to angle my chin up at will, letting my lips touch Don's as he bent down to reach for mine without that action causing me to tilt and fall over to the right.

I missed being able to hug my kids while standing upright and yelling, "May the Lord bless you and keep you, may He make is face shine on you … " as they ran out the door, only to hear them yell back, "Yeah, yeah, *I know*, Mom!"

The woman my family and friends knew and loved was mostly gone.

Someone gave me a card with a poem in it. I held it often, wondering what my life would become now that I was beginning to heal. I'd let the hope, courage, and the powerful love of God wash over me each time I read this work by a woman whose life had stopped as she'd known it in an instant.

When Pretty Things Get Broken
by Joni Eareckson Tada

I have a piece of china, a lovely porcelain vase,
It holds such lovely flowers, captures everybody's gaze.
But fragile things do slip and fall as everybody knows,
And when my vase came crashing down my tears began to flow.
But don't we all cry when pretty things get broken?
Don't we all sigh at such a loss?
But Jesus will dry those tears as he has spoken;
'Cause He was the one broken on the cross.
My life was just like China, a lovely thing to me;
It was full of porcelain promises of all that I might be.
And when my life came crashing down,
My tears began to flow.
But don't we all cry when things get broken?
Don't we all sigh at such a loss?
But Jesus will dry those tears, as he has spoken
'Cause He was the One broken on the cross.
Jesus is no porcelain Prince, His promises won't break.
His Holy Word holds fast and sure, His love, no one can shake.
So, if your life is shattered by sorrow, pain, or sin–
His healing love will reach right down and make you whole again.

Chapter
twelve

I HAD ENTERED A PLACE OF RECOVERY. MY PHYSICAL BODY HAD TURNED a corner and broken, torn parts of me were about to begin the journey of rehabilitation.

Near the end of September 1999, I decided that I'd morphed into my hospital bed at home long enough! It was time to get moving. I began what I call the *grunt work*! Someone would help me figure it out, so I had Liz phone a physiotherapist I knew. I briefly told her about the accident and the extent of my injuries, and that I was ready to go for physio.

I heard a pause and wondered if she was still there. She asked me three questions that went something like this: Can you get into a wheelchair by yourself? Can you weight bear and walk unattended? Had MPI or my OT suggested this idea to me?

Ummmmm … nope, nope, and nopers!

Cautiously, she told me she didn't believe I was ready to come for physio just yet, but she had another idea. I was all ears. She made a call.

Soon after, Jim Cathiness entered my life and our home. He came to the house three times a week through to January 2000. He'd been an employed licensed physiotherapist at HSC for years but had built his own business by going to patients in their homes. I both loved and hated him at the same time. Reminding muscles they have memory is plain old hard work. I'd say to myself, *Never, Jim!*

Jim taught me to work in the pain, through the pain, and despite the pain. I had to learn to feel the varying degrees of pain and work the muscles everywhere. He taught me to train my brain to think a certain movement long before I physically could do it. Every Monday, Wednesday, and Friday morning at ten o'clock, he took his time assessing what I could do and made me aware of what I could not do. I had grit and determination. My family said I was stubborn by refusing to admit my body couldn't do most things unassisted. (I think they called it being delusional ... grin!)

After several sessions with Jim moving my casted legs and lifting my arms forward and sideways, he asked me to think about each movement he made. He was teaching me what to feel for. After a number of assessment sessions, he positioned one arm forward and then slowly let go with his hands palms up under my elbow and wrist, saying, "Okay, now stay in this position."

Gosh, my arms weighed eight hundred pounds each! Sheesh! What happened to them? I'd sweat and tremble but concentrate not on my arm or the pain, but on the thought, *I will do this today. Today I will be able to hold this position for a few seconds.* Eventually, because muscles have memory and my brain relearned to connect with the command, I succeeded. Slowly, day by day, I'd practise until I could lift up one arm at a time—forward, sideways, and across my chest. I learned to aim for things, like a pen or napkin on the bed, and pick them up usually on the first try. (Those movements helped me hang on to a spoon to feed myself pudding!) Without moving my head even a twitch, I learned to use eye movement. Focus, aim, and pick up. That way, usually, there were only two pens or spoons moving around on the bed to try to snag. I learned to use my grabber for things not within arm's reach. I'd laugh at myself when the thing looked like a wobbly stick aimed at what seemed to be a free-floating Kleenex! I had to blow my nose, so I'd persist until I found it.

After about a month of working with Jim, he crossed his arms, stood at the end of my bed and grinned. "You've got more guts than all my patients combined. You're going to make it, you know!"

"Really?" I asked. "Really? What will that be like?"

"You've got the courage to make it," he said shaking his head. "I don't know where you get it from, but you got it."

Ah, now he was talking my language. "You really wanna know where I get courage?" I squeaked in that funny, suck-a-quick-high-breath-and-speak voice. "Jesus. Jesus, my friend, that's who."

He got that look. Lots of people I'd met since the accident had that look—respectful but disbelieving in the one who created all things. "Miracles are His specialty, don't cha know?"

Jim's eyes said, "I know she had a head injury. She's still loopy, but she does have guts. I'll not knock it in front of her, but …" Out loud he said something like, "We'll use whatever you've got, and I'll help you get better."

I smiled, gave a thumbs up to Jesus, and was grateful another agonizing physio session was over for the day. I could now rest as he shoved acupuncture needles into me for pain control. I wanted that instead of needing enough pain meds that could knock out a horse! Three times a week for many months that wonderful, faithful, and skilled man was positioned by God to teach, help, strengthen, and re-establish my body.

As Jim assessed my abilities, he pressured my orthopedist for a walking cast for my right ankle and leg. The break wasn't as severe on that side and the leg could tolerate a little weight bearing. Thus, introduction to a walker. Crutches weren't an option because they're shoved under armpits, which were connected to broken ribs and ripped upper body muscles that didn't work well. Besides, I kept tilting and falling involuntarily to the right. Jim would strap a contraption around my lower waist and hips. It had loops with a handle on the back. He'd hold me from behind—literally by my behind! I eventually learned to stand up on one casted foot, bend the left leg at the knee so the toes didn't hit the floor, and hang on to the walker's sides for dear life.

After several agonizing weeks, I made it from the bedroom to the living room, where the wheelchair was my rescue point. Shaking, exhausted, and sweating like a pig, I sat as still as possible while Jim exercised my upper body until the nausea made it impossible to continue. I'm sure he hated the thought of being barfed on whenever he came. Sometimes I wished I could, just in case it would help make the spinning world I lived in stop. Acupuncture needles for the nausea and pain sometimes helped while I'd fight to keep my eyes open, but I usually lost the battle on that one.

On and on it went. Day after endless day. Lots of family and friends came to visit, but they'd have to read a short note Liz had taped at the front door suggesting visits were to be ten to twenty minutes in length. She was a hound dog. A fresh determination to walk upright lodged in my soul.

Courage had come again: "I will learn to walk. I will learn to not fall over. I will learn to use this wheelchair and walker, but I will not stay like this forever. I will do whatever it takes to get well. I know I will. So better get out of my way, anything set against me. I will work hard, and I will walk by myself again someday!"

My life became "peat, peat, and repeat!" Strapped into my rear-end support system, being held tightly in Jim's grasp, I'd wobble down the hall to that waiting wheelchair, sit and rest, and then begin the trek back to my bed. I escaped mentally by imagining myself going for a walk in the Kananaskis Mountains in Alberta. I'd only ever driven through them, but one day … oh, I would walk those trails unassisted!

I learned to use my trusty grabber. What an excellent contraption! I could pick stuff up with it, so I didn't have to look up or down. After a while, I could even move stuff around. I celebrated each milestone with praise to my God!

Boring, you say? Yah, well, it was—but it would get me well-er and well-er!

Imagine, if you can, the freedom to be able to get in and out of the shower after months of sponge baths,. With help from Liz or Andrea, and once in a while Don, I'd slide from the wheelchair onto the medical apparatus, from which I'd then swing both legs into the tub. My upper body was strong enough to support bum walking onto the white chair suctioned to the bottom of the tub for stability. I'd get help sliding each casted leg into pliable silicone tube-like hoses and cinching them tightly. The casts stayed dry.

The first time I had clean hair in the shower felt amazing. It was a celebration when months down the road I could wash my hair all by myself. I bawled like a baby. Sheer gratitude and utter joy! I'd try to laugh, but that still hurt, so instead I gave praise in my prayer language. Often, I'd hear someone just outside the bathroom door laughing and saying something like, "There she goes again!"

I experienced freedom when I didn't need someone asking, "Are you okay?" every few minutes. The shower water running over me was often the highlight of my day. This process, however, left me utterly exhausted, so back to bed I went until the trembling, head wagging, and nausea subsided.

I learned to lie perfectly still with my eyes closed. At that stage, even the intrusive sound of a ringing telephone caused a jolt to my system. It felt like when you've had mega caffeine, and your senses are heightened, making you jump at every sound. By this time, I also had a constant ache deep in my eyes, and prickling "crawlies" up the side of my right cheek and deep into the back of my eyes. It felt much like when hand or foot "falls asleep." It hurts while you wait for the circulation to begin again.

I experienced that sensation for many years and eventually got used to it. Did I tire of that? For sure! But I refused to let it rule me. I simply assumed Jesus would help me, because He said that he would keep me. I held Him to that promise many times.

Before the accident, I prayed the way many other people did. After my trauma, however, I learned to cut prayer short and to the point. I constantly talked to God anyway. I absolutely trusted Him to keep me. He is, after all, peace, courage, hope, strength, motivator, tangible unconditional love, and always present. I know I wouldn't have survived had He not revealed Himself as faithful Abba even on the worst days, and there were many of those. On those days, I'd think of the children's book, *Alexander and the Terrible, Horrible, No Good, Very Bad Day* by Judith Viorst.

I'm glad Jesus taught me a lesson that stuck early on during recovery and rehabilitation. Cornerstone-Hillsong recorded a song with the lyrics: "My hope is built on nothing less than Jesus's blood and righteousness. I dare not trust the sweetest frame but wholly trust in Jesus's name." This old hymn is rooted in the Word of God and makes many references to Jesus alone as righteous and our only hope.

If I had moved in hope that my body would be able to perform certain tasks and then didn't, I would have become a despairing, hopeless creature indeed! My hope was to be in Jesus Christ alone. Period. No matter what my body did or did not do, or what life was like for me here on this earth, I would trust Him.

My hope and faith were also not in my prayers or the prayers of others. They were *in* the Holy One who heard each prayer. Besides, He answered them! After all, He had said He would keep me. Sigh … that wasn't always an easy cakewalk! But a courage deep inside grew, and I became fearless.

Woe to anyone who got in the way of my recovery, much to the chagrin of my family at times!

* * *

The first part of the year after being whacked about in that car, every day was the same. Slowly I'd become aware that I was waking up. I'd learned never to open my eyes right away, and I didn't move a muscle, twitch, or yawn. Every inch of me hurt, inside and out. However, a full bladder doesn't like to be kept waiting. I'd take three shallow breaths through the nose, exhale slowly through mouth, and lift one arm slowly forty-five degrees up and then lower, repeating on other side. I'd clench my fists and pump blood into circulation before doing three to five bum pinches slowly. Next, I'd slide the foot across the bed sheet, bend my knee, and let my leg slide down to touch floor. Then I'd coax the other leg to follow. These movements brought the familiar, ever-present nausea and a head that felt like it was bobbing around like a kids' toy in a swimming pool.

Still, nature called. My job was to get my eyes to stay open long enough to fixate on one spot on the wall to slow down the spinning sensation. Then inch by inch to roll onto my right side (Never left ... nasty broken ribs, remember?) while simultaneously using gut muscles and my right elbow on the bed to push my upper body into sitting position. During this time, I used my left hand to push left leg to greet the right knee dangling over the side. Finally, inch by agonizing inch, I got to sit on a now very full bladder. When the forward swaying to the right began, I'd reach out and grab the arm of the locked wheelchair, which had been correctly positioned the night before.

Repetition and continuous practice over eight months had enabled me to get into the wheelchair all alone. Independence and victory. Wow! Now I had to push myself across the hall, perform similar movements, and haul my now-little butt on the toilet! I experienced trembling, shaky success. This went on for months until little by little I became a pro. My upper body muscles got stronger as I healed and used them regularly. My ankles knit together under those casts, and I gained strength to bear some weight on both legs. Today I am in awe of how many muscles God created for the purpose of a person's morning routine.

I explain this daily routine because it was the stepping stone I used to build up endurance for living. I had learned to persevere and would need dogged determination to relearn how to do many ordinary things. Everybody knows that what goes up must come down, and so it was for my daily morning routine. Every morning I had to methodically backtrack so I could get back to my safest haven—my bed.

I repeated that activity again and again and again until I no longer wanted to drink any fluids! There were days I simply didn't make it to the washroom. Humiliating for sure, but by then all dignity had been blown out of the water, and I didn't care. I wanted the grey place of escape, but instead I'd gasp and long for the pain to stop. Just *stop*. I'd mentally throw up my hands in despair. All I did was "run" to Jesus like a child into Daddy's arms, and *be*. I'd huddle and be still. No time to think about "ascending to the hill of the Lord!" I just ran to where I knew I was safe to only exist. Jesus would rescue me by soothing my body as I rested until next time.

The repeated bed exercises, isometric stretches, acupuncture, and assisted-walker walking gave me increased strength. Learning to concentrate step by step and walk on casted legs using a walker created confidence.

* * *

By mid-October, I'd made a decision. Our son, Aaron, was marrying Wilma on November 6, 1999, and I was *not* going to have those ugly neon-green casts sticking out of the elegant mother-of-the-groom dress Wilma and I had chosen one week before the MVA. (How about *that* for the provision of God! I was in no shape to go shopping. I even had my shoes!) My selfless seamstress friend, Hanni, came over to hem that dress the moment she heard of my plan.

I decided to ask my multitalented, beautiful friend Donna to help with wedding arrangements. She gladly set aside two weeks of her life to get all the things done I couldn't do for my kids. I struggled to design one stunning pew bow, which she somehow multiplied into many! My faithful sister, Betty, said that she'd take care of helping the bridal party get ready at her house. The guys would get dressed at our place. They didn't need help! I often wept alone at night because I keenly felt the loss of not being a part of all the hoopla like I could have been had the MVA not happened.

I didn't divulge my plan to walk down that wedding aisle to my family. Two weeks before the wedding, I had talked to my orthopedist and told him that I wasn't going to walk down the aisle at my son's wedding in casts and with a walker. I wanted those casts off now! He was rather dubious, but I convinced him that my ankles would never get stronger sitting in those stinky casts forever. I was sick and tired of the itch! I wanted them off ... that day ... oh, and by the way, *please*!

Reluctantly he agreed but insisted I leave with "air casts" on both ankles, and a pair of the ugliest fitted orthopedic shoes you ever saw. I had to promise not to weight bear for more than a minute or two at a time. Done! I think I floated out the hospital doors in my wheelchair, ready to get on with walking by myself! A regular Chitty Chitty Bang Bang ... giggling away!

At home I showed off my new and improved casts and tried to model my new freedom with those ugly shoes. My family laughed with me because we all knew I'd never win an award on a model's runway. Who cared? I could stand up and take a step!

Romans 12:12 helped me focus on being grateful and hopeful instead of on how much my body hurt: *"Be glad for all God is planning for you. Be patient in trouble, and prayerful always"* (TLB).

Jim still came three times per week. He showed me new exercises and new ways to move. I mastered them all and more. I was on a mission. My resolve to walk down that aisle for our son grew stronger.

Several times a day, when everyone was gone and Liz thought I was resting, I'd practise walking. I'd inch my way along the bed to the window by myself. I'd then hang on to that window ledge for dear life until I could gently raise my heel off the floor and not fall over.

I had decided that I could walk down that aisle with air casts in those new shoes and light a candle, which Aaron would later blow out, symbolizing that his time as a single son was over. On November 6, 1999, I felt proud and grateful to have Don slowly help me accomplish this small thing. We often laughed that it was a good thing that Don, as a former police officer, was skilled at helping a drunk walk! Even though I had practised like crazy, I was still as wobbly as if I'd downed a whole bottle of wine.

Many tears of joy flowed that day as we shared with family and friends in the beginning of Aaron and Wilma's new life together. I had used every fibre of my being to make it to the wedding, and by mid-November I hit what is known as the WALL. No surprise, but it was unlike anything I'd experienced before. Mental health professionals have endless ways to describe this wall of trauma, which takes many different forms.

By now I was able to make my own coffee in the morning *if* every little thing to make it was laid out for me within a reachable distance of my wheelchair. I no longer needed care 24/7. I liked being more independent. I was totally sideswiped when I got to the kitchen one morning and felt everything start to go black. I remember wheeling to the kitchen table to hang on and put my head down so I wouldn't fall to the floor. I was alone in the house.

My experience with that kind of trauma hit me—mind, body, and spirit—all at the same time. I saw and felt huge, horrible, unstoppable tsunami waves of black heavy water rolling toward me, and I was sure they would kill me. They kept coming closer and closer, and I couldn't stop them from drowning me. As this power overtook me, I heard myself whisper the name of Jesus and then briefly recognized His light far away.

I heard a dreadful sound come out of me—a keening, wailing sound that went on and on and on. It subsided, and then as the black wall of water swallowed me, I heard a louder, more agonizing wailing build to a deafening peak. Somewhere in there I realized that those horrible sounds were coming out of my mouth. I didn't fight it or try to stop the unstoppable. I felt frozen. Immobile. I have no recollection of how long it lasted, but eventually I felt the hand of God surround me and pull me through into the light I had seen in the distance.

When I became aware of myself, I was at the kitchen table and sopping wet. My hair was soaked. Dripping with sweat from head to toe, the shaking began. I felt myself slide down out of the wheelchair and onto the floor, shivering. That's how Liz found me that day. She gently washed me all over—and I do mean everywhere. She never said a word but tucked me into bed. The liquid gold I had repeatedly seen in the hospital filled our bedroom. I saw that same humongous white angel I'd seen before lean against the wall by the door, and I felt completely loved and safe. I went into a deep sleep. I don't know how long I slept, but the next morning, I called the MPI adjuster and asked for a psychiatrist or psychologist who was also a believer in the power of God, because He had just pulled me through the trauma wall.

That's how I met a young man, Dr. Ian Mogilevsky. Together, he and I began a different kind of therapy. What a godly blessing in human form! I say, "Thank you, Father, yet again, for opening the door for this child of God to help one you came to save—me!"

Chapter
Thirteen

By November 1999, a week before Aaron and Wilma's wedding, I was more mobile than the day of the MVA the previous July! I was a determined patient, getting well from home with all kinds of medical and family help. I was sweating and working my buns off to get better. Because my desire to become well was great, I orally presented myself better than I actually was. Only my family and Liz saw the real struggles and lowest times. That was to my detriment. Insurance companies have a kah-zillion policies that make up more policies and rigid grids that their insurance adjusters, nurse employees, and assessment doctors must adhere to. They are not there to be your therapist. They are an insurance company, and care costs money.

Now that I was upright, could weight bear for a few minutes, sort of walk independently with a walker without always tipping or falling, be in a wheelchair for short periods of time unattended, and feed myself fairly well when food was placed in front of me, I was deemed fit enough to not need homecare any longer.

An insurance-employed, binder-toting nurse was sent to our house about a week before Aaron and Wilma's wedding date. She hardly looked at me but looked around our home and stated rather sarcastically that I sure had it made. She hauled out her binder and firmly stated that things were about to change. She never asked about how I had gotten to the place of wellness I now presented. She told me I looked great and not sick at all sitting my wheelchair. After all, I didn't have any little children to take care of, and Don, Andrea, or that newly-married son of mine and his wife could clean the house and cook—even though they all worked all day and often into the evenings. She didn't care if I could open the fridge door or pour anything into a cup. This insurance nurse had been sent to assess and gather all the evidence needed to stop homecare help. I'd had help for four months since leaving the hospital, and there were others in far worse shape than I. She ticked box after box in that folder and stated that I no longer fell into the grid of needing homecare. If I wanted help like that to continue, I'd have to pay someone.

She raised her eyebrow at me and suggested that, had I opted to go to the Sherbrooke Rehab Centre straight from the trauma ward and stayed there like I should have, all of my body's needs would have been met there, and MPI would only have been involved after I got home. They would, however, provide a house cleaning service every two weeks. She snapped her binder shut, looked at Liz to tell her she'd be reassigned, and marched out the door.

Sweet, caring, no-nonsense Liz took my hand and, with tears in her eyes, told me she'd be staying to help me until after the wedding. She did. We reimbursed her for the time she took off from other work. Sometimes she showed up without us even asking.

There was no transition time. Rude reality check! I began to wish I had stayed at HSC, because it would have been easier on my family. They could have just come to visit and then go home and live normally. It was hard on them and me.

I began to feel like a serious burden to them. They didn't want me to feel like that, but I did, especially since I was now well enough to think. I realized how sick I'd been, what the accident had done, and the horrible fear they'd experienced. I sagged inside the day I became aware that I'd been home for months and hadn't been able to take care of anyone or anything for all that time.

I was also scared by the fact that my memory wasn't working right. That was frustrating, especially for Don. Others' ineptitude had always been a source of great irritation for him. Now it was me—the woman he loved. I still looked like me—thinner and gaunt—but I was different. He tried to be patient but struggled.

Often, I'd cry myself to sleep at night—me upstairs in my button-pushing bed, and Don in our basement on our queen-size mattress. I was extremely lonely, feeling like a burden, and definitely not a beautiful or sexy wife. The sadness of grieving the loss of who I was had become unbearable. I wanted to run away from my body and be free to fly like Don still could … he could go out and away to work.

* * *

I continued physio three times a week with Jim at the house as November rolled over to December. It was an unusual but deeply meaningful Christmas that year, full of thanks and gratitude. It was also the funniest, fastest Christmas shopping trip in our marriage's history! Don took me, list in hand. Pushing that wheelchair in the mall gave him a sense of power. Sheesh! He was in control of the contraption I sat in! He'd never had that kind of power before. I grinned the whole time, I think. I was at his mercy, and he could go into whatever store he wanted, and I had to go too. Needless to say, our Christmas shopping got done in about three hours flat! My job had been to hold the Christmas shopping list, make sure I'd taken enough pain meds to stay "with it" and a anti-nausea pill called Maxeran so the spinning in my head stayed manageable. It was the first time he and I had had a fun-filled day since the accident.

In January 2000, rehab turned a corner and super-serious work began. Jim handed my file to the PAR unit (Prevention, Assessment, and Rehabilitation) at the H.S. Rehabilitation Centre. That dear man had helped start me on my new life.

Every Monday, Wednesday, and Friday I'd go through the process of getting out of bed as nausea rolled in. During this stage of recovery, I was thankful MPI provided a handicap van. I'd go through the bathroom routine, get dressed, and make my way into the wheelchair. Gullwing Transport would arrive at 9:30 a.m., so I'd be at the centre by 10:00. At first just getting there, being there, and gratefully leaving was awful. Awful is just that. Awful.

I began several months of gruelling physical workouts, with or without mechanical devices to help me get out of the chair. I also endured physio treatments and acupuncture for pain control. I'd lie perfectly still at the end of each session as one of the wonderful staff tucked hot or cold packs as needed. I learned to separate myself and not hear or feel anything by falling into Jesus, where I was safe, at rest, and occasionally pain free. In that place, I'd remember songs or phrases to help me. Mostly, though, I'd silently pray in my prayer language, because I didn't want some analyst called in to see if I was delusional! I was used to talking to my Jesus that way.

Since I was always dizzy, nauseous, and off balance, I was introduced to vestibular physio down the hall from PAR. That began a relationship with Beth Wonnick, who ran the department. She was a fabulous Christian woman who knew what she was doing by making me use a bunch of eye and head movements to train my brain to tell my body to stay upright. She also made me good and sick every single time—nauseous and wobbly for the next eight months, twice a week! What fun that was! I liked her but hated the vestibular physio.

After months of this, I overheard another patient talk about going for a walk in the tunnels underneath the hospital that connected various departments. It's a different world down there. I decided to gain upper body strength on my own down there. I never told a soul what I was doing. I'd leave my gym bag with one of the PAR physios before going for vestibular physio and then hit the tunnels. I discovered that the tunnels were the "bowels of the ship" at HSC. They went on for miles. The laundry room was down there, along with huge pipes connecting everything, transport tractor type things, people who pushed equipment from place to place, and the morgue. I lost count of the number of times I either got lost or was too exhausted to backtrack to the entry door. God always sent someone to help navigate me back to rehab. I became stronger in my upper body, and I was *free* while I was down there. No one asked or told me to do anything. I loved that place of respite. It was my secret.

Rolling forward in my wheelchair through those tunnels strengthened my resolve. I didn't care how far I pushed, huffed, puffed, sweated, and glided, just as long as I could make it back to the elevator and up to where the sun shone and Gullwing Transport came to take me home again—home to those I loved and appreciated more and more.

My family loved me and cheered me on. In the past, love had been conditional in our family at times. Now, more often the love and acceptance of each other grew as we each navigated personal "tunnels" knowing that

Jesus was right there. We were where God already was. There is no place we can go that God has not already gone. God is who He says He is—sovereign.

Learning to "ride in the tunnels" that winter would have been such a waste if we, as a family, had become bitter because of what the accident had done to us. Instead, God showed us day by day, often in movement, experience, or events, how to become better. For us, it meant praying and being happy just to be. There weren't many strings attached to stuff or material things, and we didn't particularly care about people's opinions or advice. That attitude helped us accept others— "Cause that's where they are right now," or "Gosh, they sure do need to be right about a lot, don't they?"

Some folks struggled with what to say or how to be when healing came at a snail's pace; some felt they had to offer advice, or were confused that their prayers for me had not yet been answered, but the ones closest to us loved on us as we found a new way to be as a family.

We learned to take pleasure in and celebrate moments and milestones, big and small. I love the verse in Zechariah 4:10a, where I'm told, "*Do not despise these small beginnings, for the Lord rejoices to see the work begin, to see the plumb line …*" First Corinthians 12:12–26 provides a picture of how the church, the body of Christ, is to function. Verse twelve says, "*The human body has many parts, but the many parts make up one whole body. So it is with the body of Christ.*"

After the accident, my "body parts" changed. I got to live this out first within my own physical body, then within the structure of our own family, and eventually as a part of the body of Christ. Things change, but each part offered has value no matter what shape it's in.

Chapter
fourteen

I TREASURED MOMENTS WITH DON. HE WAS NEVER AT EASE SITTING beside my bed and talking unless we had something important to discuss. I couldn't tell him how it really was for me those early months, because then I'd have to deal with his anger at whoever or whatever had caused my distress. He badly wanted to get this whole mess (me and the accident) fixed. To sit quietly at my bedside, relax, and *just be* was rare at first. I was too sick to care. I wasn't able to take care of me, and he was on his own.

He'd never truly had to take care of the kids and me emotionally or spiritually. I'd been that primary caregiver, while he'd been a wonderful provider and let's-get-this-done guy. Now that "me" was gone and needed the nurturing. I didn't have the energy to think about being sorry for him.

One day God showed me something, and I knew what He said was true. I had to talk with Don about it. That night after he came in to say goodnight, I said, "Don, most couples who go through this kind of trauma don't make it. Most of them get divorced. Are we going to do that too?"

He teared up and for the first time his dam broke. We both wept for our loss. We didn't just cry about it … we wept. He moved in as close and he could, and I attempted to sit forward, trying with all I had in me not to shake and tremble too badly. Together, we were simply sad for a long time that night.

We decided to get good, godly counsel from psychologist Dr. Bill Davis. We were determined not to become a divorce stat. We chose to learn how to live one day at a time, whatever that looked like. We started to focus and began a rehabilitation of our wounded emotions. It's true that whatever we focus on, we empower. We made up our minds to empower one another in this new way of living, and Jesus was with us all the time.

We began making bi-weekly trips into the heart of downtown Winnipeg. For me, it meant getting there and back using Gullwing Transport Services sent by their wonderful dispatcher. For Don, it meant finding his own parking, meeting me in the lobby, and wheeling me to the elevator and to Dr. Davis's office.

Getting out of the house and down those icy ramps in Manitoba's winter was crazy—not fun! I was sweating and exhausted by the time I'd had help getting dressed and my coat on. What a lengthy process, and not even out the door! Then the ride … ah, the ride, with the wheelchair locked in behind the Gullwing van driver. Each driver was unique and had a different style. They were amazing and knew how to manoeuvre me without too much trouble. Both legs and feet were still casted, and both had to be elevated, otherwise those ol' casts seemed to shrink in size. Not too comfy! Now Don had something he could do. He helped me get in and out of that psychologist's office without banging my feet on any walls.

We had decided that in order to survive, we had to learn how to live with how it was. Our past was now the past, and we really only had the one day we were in. How to live now?

Slowly, painfully, one session at a time, Dr. Davis helped us discover what we had lost, what we wanted to re-establish, what was good to leave in the past, and how to discover who Don and Hedy wanted to be now. What kind of marriage relationship did we want? In what ways could we be different, as we now needed new tools of relating? Many of our old ones were broken, rusted out, or just plain useless. Slowly our new toolbox began to emerge. It was the grace of God that led us to this rehab and a great kindness toward one another that kept us from throwing in the towel and living separate, wounded lives under the same roof.

We discovered that being in love would carry us through to learning to love one another one day at a time through the many changes. To quit was not an option. True love was re-kindled, and an excitement for the future emerged. After all, we were both on the same ancient, blood-bought path paved by Jesus, and we'd both asked the Holy Spirit to indwell and lead us. Jesus had saved me from myself by forgiving my sins years before, and Don had given his heart over to Jesus in 1998, a year before the accident. He'd been baptized that spring. What a celebration of rejoicing that day was for our family. What's not to like about that!

As Don learned to feel, he also learned the difference between verbally aggressive self-preservation and the assertive behaviour that gets you to a better place. That takes thought and practice.

I learned to try to listen and then think. After thinking, I'd know what I was feeling and could say in a short sentence what normally would have taken me ages to get out. I practised thinking what I was thinking about. Sometimes I was sure I could feel steam rising out of my ears while I kept my mouth shut and listened!

We began to get better at listening with our ears and hearing with our hearts. It was the kindness of God that let us feel this kind of sorrow, pain, and loss so that we'd be able to move forward together at the same time. Today I believe with all my heart that listening is an art. It takes a lifetime of two people willing to do whatever it takes, for however long.

At the time, I sanctimoniously believed that I had it more together than Don. After all, I heard God and saw angels. Ouch. Imagine that! How arrogant of me. I'd been learning humility in having others help me with every little thing physically, and now it was time to learn to house the humility of my Lord and Saviour Jesus Christ in my spirit.

It was emotional and spiritual work to get well together, but it was amazing to begin to believe that we could do anything in order to help ourselves. Helpless ways slowly became moments of hopeful restoration. Don learned that he had not always loved me as he ought. I learned that I had definitely not always respected him like I ought. We had to put pride, anger, fear, and frustration back at Jesus's feet and ask Him to help us forgive. We wanted to know how to do that together, to be in that place of beginning to live in joyful restoration.

Chapter *fifteen*

My recovery story may be unusual because Jesus Christ made Himself known to me all the time and not only when I asked. I never felt abandoned or wondered where He was. I don't know why I was blessed in this way, but I was. With every turn and twist of recovery during rehab, Jesus was my best cheerleader. That's why I wasn't surprised when God spoke to me again in June 2000 while coming home in a smelly taxi from a grueling workout at HSC Rehab Center.

I was overextended, in pain, and mentally done. I opened the cab window for fresh air, looked out, sagged and said, "I can't do this one more day Jesus. I can't!" It was then He spoke out loud, "There's a place deep inside called Courage and (His Voice paused) someday it will be a book." I glanced at the cab driver thinking he heard God too, but he was on his phone. Tears quietly flowed as I whispered, "Well then, Jesus, you better fix me." And fix me He did!

As new forms of physical therapy were introduced, practised, and mastered, I knew He was pleased with me, much as a father is "proud as punch" of his kid. I knew His pleasure. "*The Lord takes pleasure in those who fear Him, in those who hope in His mercy*" (Psalm 147:11, NKJV). It wasn't a matter of getting it right or finishing well. Jesus was always present, and I knew His pleasure. I was in complete awe of holy God.

Knowing God's pleasure gave me the guts to hit those "tunnels" without telling anyone. I knew people would block my recovery at times like that. That's why I'd pray in tongues as I pushed myself. Those who heard me muttering and mumbling often said, "Whatever works for ya." Jesus, my cheerleader, shouted through the noisy din of those tunnels one day in the form of a maintenance worker: "Way to go, lady!" Sometimes He used a worker to push my wheelchair back to the elevators, because I'd obviously run out of steam. Yup, those tunnels became the nitty gritty of Jesus, Christ in me, the hope of glory for the church, and getting 'er done.

By early spring of 2000, my upper body muscles grew stronger and I began to take care of my personal needs. What bliss to be in a bathroom unattended without hearing, "Are you okay in there?" What a relief for my family not to constantly wonder if I'd fallen off the toilet seat or slid off the bench in the shower and couldn't get out.

In time, more than a few odd things became apparent due to my head injury. My brain didn't compute well, so I often was unaware of these oddities. I didn't know I couldn't do something until I tried and it didn't work. What a shock to think you can but can't. It reminded me of Aaron, who at five years old thought that the first time he put on skates and got on the ice, he'd skate like Wayne Gretzky! A look of utter disbelief and shock played across his cute face. His incorrect assumption knocked him right on his little keister! That's how I felt many times! I learned to relearn how to do countless ordinary things.

For example, one morning on my "day off," everyone was out of the house. Alone, I thought, *I feel like eating a boiled egg.* Piece a cake, right? Wrong!

Hedy's Recipe for One Boiled Egg after a Whack on the Head

Method:
Manoeuvre out of bed and into wheelchair. Wheel down hallway to kitchen wondering where to search for a cooking pot. Oops—way down at the bottom of that cupboard. Can't reach. Wheel back to bedroom, get trusty ol' grabber. Wheel back to kitchen. Snafu pot lid and lift on counter. Fandangle pot and try to lift onto lap. Try again and again and again. Success.

Mixing:
Manoeuvre out of locked wheelchair. Hang on to kitchen counter at sink. Stand on good leg and turn on tap water. Slide pot

over and fill in sink. Too heavy! Rats! Dump out some water. Think, *Where's the egg?* Manoeuvre back into wheelchair.

Good tip: Position wheelchair on side of fridge door so you reach in and not around. Remember grabber if needed to pull out egg carton onto lap in one smooth, concentrated movement. Very important step for the success of one boiled egg. Don't drop. If sweating and shaking too badly, rest. Close eyes and don't give up.

Resume task. Place carton on counter first. Don't take egg out and try to stand up with open carton on lap. Eggs roll off counter. Put directly into pot of water in sink.

Execution:

While standing on one leg, lift pot out of that sink with both hands onto counter and sit back into wheelchair. Transfer pot with egg and water from counter to lap.

Oh darn. Can't lift pot from wheelchair position. Can't hold pot with one hand; need two. Can't get it to the stove element without spilling. Return pot to sink and let it spill inside. Oh well—have a boiled egg later when someone else is home.

Wheel back to bed, sweating, still hungry, and exhausted.

Later Andrea asked, "Did you try to boil an egg for yourself?"

I drew a blank. "Don't think so." I'd completely forgotten that I'd tried.

The End

Another day down the road of recovery. It was *boring* and about to become frustrating. This methodical thought process of left brain connecting successfully with the right brain took me to a completely new level of relearning what I had once known. I had to learn to catch thoughts and keep them so I could use them.

Today I can whip up a boiled egg and make a mean egg salad sandwich in no time flat! The repeated efforts to do sequential steps taught me to think using brain muscle memory. The children's story of *The Little Engine that Could* (by Watty Piper) is true. I spent years chugging uphill, saying, "I think I can. I think I can. I think I can ... boil an egg," or some such thing.

Now many years later—dang! That egg salad I made by myself tastes fabulous. Like the *Little Engine that Could*, I too, "thought I could, I thought I could!" Today, I ask, "Can I make you one, or would you like to share mine?" Simple pleasures are wonderful all by themselves. They become even more wonderful when they are shared.

I expected Jesus to show up and help while I thought or did something. He was also present when I was simply me, not doing much of anything. I never had to wait for Him to show up. Ever. He was already where I had been and was where I'd be going. My Jesus, my forever friend. Thank you ... egg-zact-ly!

* * *

In May 2008, I wrote a story for my husband for Father's Day. He had told a story about himself as a kid to a truly good friend. He retold it to me and—*ding*—I secretly wrote his story and kicked it up a notch for the special day. With tears in his eyes as he read, Don looked straight at me and said, "Hedy, you really ought to make this one into a children's book."

"Sure, Don," I said flippantly. "If God drops an editor *and* a publisher on my head at the same time, I'll do it!"

Well, and don't ya know ... God did ... two weeks later, *and* an illustrator to boot! That's how my Father's Day gift turned into a true story about my hubby. I fictionalized it and that version became a published children's story. We called it *Donnie's Little Red Wagon*. It was published by Forever Books. What an adventure that has been for us as a couple. It turned out to be a wonderful reprieve from the medical abyss my life had become. Life was no longer a daily marathon, and times of relational restoration were sweet.

Chapter
sixteen

THEN THERE WERE *THOSE* DAYS, CALL THEM WHAT YOU WILL. THEY were awful, bad, crappy, horrible, achy, fog-filled, pain-filled, just plain "let's delete" days.

On those days a discontent would creep deep into my soul, and the reality of how hard my life really was took over in some form. Sometimes irritability rose up, and I'd be plain snarky with whoever was there. Sometimes I felt anger at parts of my body that either weren't functioning well or always hurting, making me zone out or check out mentally. I let myself feel angry without any guilt at all.

The zone-out method worked when the dizzies and nausea were especially tiresome and I had to stop moving. At those times, hand signals either worked out or brought more confusion. At times I was so self-absorbed, I'd become sick of myself and hide. It's called close the door— a real door with a knob, or the door of my mind or heart. Just exist—for a bit.

The worst feeling, though, was being sad. I never fought against any of these emotions. I let them come, probably because I didn't have the energy to fight back. All my strength was used to try to get well. Combine all that with learning to use a wheelchair, walk, walk on two casts and not fall over, and—AHRGH! What a tiresome mess! At times during those years of healing, thoughtless people would ask, "So … what do you do all day?"

I learned to say, "I work full-time! I work at getting well!"

I wrote a poem on one of those day when I was simply unable to keep up with all the able-bodied people in my life. Not my finest hour for sure!

Don't Come Near Me

Don't come near me—
I'm in a rush!
I've no time for you.
I'm in the Devil's Push!
It feels so good to always go—
I must provide now, don't cha know?
The time I have is not enough.
I think my God helps me be tough.
I use His strength at each new day
To serve myself, my work, avoiding play.
Don't tell me that I don't listen
Ignoring those eyes with tears that glisten-
I've no time to stop for you
So, don't come near me now
I've things to do!
I'm sure sorry, but—
I've just got no time for you.

On those days I learned to wait, just be, ask for help or a hug, try to read, hope for a friend to call or visit, tell someone what I wanted or needed … a, b, c, or d. Mostly, though, I'd wait it out, knowing beyond any doubt that somehow Jesus would come to me. He always did. Somehow or in some way. I sure didn't always pray or ask or lean on or trust. I just was, and He was too. Without fail, He'd come to me. I'd hear Him in my heart or He'd come in my thoughts with whatever He knew I needed. Usually He came in people. He loved using people so I could see and touch Him. There were countless times when someone in my family, or a friend, showed up with a distraction.

I no longer asked Jesus, "How did you do that?" Most often I felt a wonderful physical warmth flow over my whole body, much like an ocean wave. It would roll over my everything and suck me into Him, taking off or out of me all the stuff of the day(s). I'd been given His presence. I didn't have language, words, or a whole lot of intellectual thought. I simply knew my heavenly Father in that place of His keeping again, and He was enough.

The days or moments of "so awful" had been changed, because He had come to me. He was faithful. I could rest, try again, and get better day by day, week by week, month by month, and now year by year. I know Christ as Courage. He doesn't simply give courage, or teach me how to be courageous, or have me exercise courage. No. He gives me courage to live and discover what my God intends. He fills me. Courage has enabled me to become uncluttered so as to be relentlessly pursued plus deeply and utterly consumed by the love of God.

Chapter
seventeen

BY ALLOWING MYSELF TO UNDERTAKE THE TEDIOUS PROCESS OF remembering how the various stages of rehabilitation and recovery unfolded, I became overwhelmed with the realization that all I knew about the actual accident was what others had told me. My body experienced two more full-blown episodes of immobilizing, drowning trauma. With good counselling and therapy advice, I needed to go back so I could go forward. I needed to see for myself. I learned to drive again.

On July 31, 2000, a year after the accident, I decided to go back and revisit that day for real. I drove to the crash site alone. I didn't know what my body would do, but I trusted Jesus to keep me. Let me give you a glimpse into why there is that place deep inside I call Courage:

* * *

I drive to the crash site, see the intersection where it happened. I pull off Highway 8 and onto a side road to park the car on the gravel. I get out using my two canes for support and shakily make my way down into the ditch where the mangled wrecks had landed. I'm standing in the grass between two highways, the one going north, the other south. The one going north is the one where traffic roars by at break-neck speeds of over a hundred kilometres an hour. The highway where a gigantic red sign screams *Stop* to any and all within its visual radius.

I stand staring at the sign and the traffic. My eyes hurt because the brightness of the Manitoba sun is beating down. It's hot … oh so hot. But that's nothing compared to what's happening inside of me.

After getting myself to this spot, *the spot* in the grass that's growing in the ditch, my eyes blink involuntarily as my mind, body, and spirit react to what I'm told happened here. I cannot remember—even that ability was stolen. My whole life screeched to a halt that day on July 31, 1999.

Organic amnesia is the inability to have any memory because of being in a totally unconscious state. That's why I stand here staring at the grass and see broken bits of a rear tail light, a pink piece of torn leather, a twisted fender, a syringe, a dried, bloody surgical rubber glove. There are deep gouges in the ground where new grass is trying to grow to cover old paint, scattered screws, dried, ripped parts of a book, a notebook, a blue piece of metal.

I realize what Don said is truth. This is a graveyard. This is where he made himself go right after the accident to search for my eyeglasses, broken to bits just like me. A place where only a little bit remains as a reminder of the crash. I see the smashed, crushed, horrific remains of our collision and many others. In my mind, I can hear metal to metal screeching as vehicles collide, leaving devastation in their wake.

I stare at the stop sign, imagining it as I'm told it happened. I let myself "see" a young mother, hurried and distracted. She's turning her head and looking away from the road. She's speeding toward the intersection where the huge sign shrieks *Stop*! She's out of control in her heart, so she's yelling at the little four-year-old daughter who is unbuckled from her seatbelt. The girl stands behind her mother's seat. They drive a maroon van. The mom is ignoring the road sign. She doesn't slow down much. She sees the stop sign but instantly decides she can "beat the traffic" and quickly cross the highway without stopping. She makes a huge mistake.

Her carelessness is why I now stand sweating and shaking in the heat, on the grass, in the car's graveyard. Staring because I've given myself permission to feel, to allow my mind, body, and spirit to do whatever is necessary for me to get well. I'm not surprised or appalled at the hot- white surge of rage that suddenly, for the first time in a year, courses through every fibre of my being. *Stupid!* my mind screams, *Stupid! Stupid! Stupid! What a stupid thing. The accident should never have happened. Stupid!* The rage within me bursts forth and out of my mouth. "What a stupid woman! This accident was so unnecessary!"

I become aware of who came with me. The One I'd invited to be with me—Jesus. My weakening body no longer wants to stay upright, despite the aid of two supporting canes, one in each hand. *I've got to get back to my car.*

Slowly, mechanically, my physical body responds. One painful step at a time I leave that graveyard, for I know that back in my parked car I can sit down *in* the One who is safe. My Jesus has promised to keep me. To keep me forever and until …

Back inside my car and into the reality of that time, my awareness is only of Christ, my friend. I faintly hear traffic and feel the heat of the day elevating the temperature inside the vehicle, but I feel His nearness more intensely than the heat outside. Spirit to spirit.

The language of His Spirit resonates within me as He begins talking to my spirit. I respond. How can I not? The language is not my mother tongue but utterings of the Spirit. This language in prayer is physically audible on my part, yet Jesus speaks only to my heart. I know, hear, and recognize His voice, for His voice is supernatural. That's why it's not unusual for me to allow the outflowing of my innermost part. Up my gut and through my throat come the familiar, strange-sounding utterances of my spirit. He knows me oh so well. I'm glad to have been one of His sheep for years!

I quietly breathe, "Hello, I'm home."

And He responds, "I know, my little one, I know."

Being guided by Jesus through what feels like a maze is surreal; it's not natural. It is, in fact, supernatural because it is done in the Spirit, led by the Holy Spirit, with revelation imparted because the Spirit of the living God decrees it is to be done in a life.

While in my car, I am given comfort, and I know I must open my Bible. I shakily read Isaiah 51, beginning with verse twelve: "*I, yes I, am the one who comforts you. So why are you afraid of mere humans, who wither like the grass and disappear?*"

I reply honestly, "Because I hate being in pain, and she was human."

I continue to read "*Yet you* (Hedy) *have forgotten the Lord, your Creator, the one who stretched out the sky like a canopy and laid the foundations of the earth. Will you remain in constant dread of human oppressors?*" (Isaiah 51:13a).

"Father," I whisper, "no. No I won't."

I continue to read, "Will you continue to fear the anger of your enemies?"

"I didn't know I have enemies. Who are they?" I ask.

Again, I hear His voice plainly, clearly, from within. He speaks truth. "The intentions of the evil one is against you."

"But," I counter, "I am in your keeping. You promised. You *promised*!"

The silence causes me to continue reading in Isaiah. "*Soon all you captives will be released! Imprisonment, starvation, and death will not be your fate!*" (v. 14).

"Thank you, Lord. Forgive me. Forgive me for wavering even for a while. I know that all the things of the Spirit are eternally safe and well. You are the guarantee for safety. You are the One alone!"

I continue with a fresh determination: "I now, in Jesus's name, leave the power of the dread behind me to be dealt with according to the justice of my God."

In that instant, I know that I know that I know I have left the "power of the dread" behind. Behind. Back in the place where it took place. Now tears flow, but they are tears of a different kind.

Relief floods me briefly as I try to see the Word through my tears. "*For I am the Lord your God, who stirs up the sea, causing its waves to roar. My name is the Lord of Heaven's Armies*" (v. 15).

I weep, sobbing deeply with complete relief. "Oh good, Lord! Good! So good! So good!"

Once more I'm aware of the intense heat of the day. I open a window, and the traffic sounds accost my ears. It feels like someone slapped me. I quickly roll up the window, unwilling to be invaded. I'm stunned when a profound heaviness settles over, around, and all the way through me, almost like a huge wet wave. It feels like I'm being covered by water, yet I breathe. Scared, all I can say is, "Oh Jesus, oh Jesus, oh Jesus." It's all I'm capable of.

Tears turn into sobbing again. A wailing lament erupts as the last of the hot rage begins to be transformed by the Spirit of my loving God. Jesus and me. Just Jesus and me. The wailing increases; I can hear myself—howling, keening, lamenting the violation of my body and mind, just because one mother made a terrible, careless mistake that very nearly cost me my life.

"The cost is too high!" my mind yells at me, and instantaneously my heart hears my Keeper. "My life cost Me everything."

The tumultuous waves of emotion begin to recede. Slowly, so slowly, I realize I'm alive in my car. I'm present and somewhat aware of sounds … crunching gravel as another car passes mine.

As I wade through the tidal waves of emotion that kind of trauma brings, I come to a pivotal moment when my Lord commands loudly, "Forgive her."

His voice silences all. Everything! I could choose. I thought I had. I'd said the words before. I knew if I chose not to forgive, that precious part of me called my soul would die too—then all of the me I had known would be gone. Sitting, head bowed, once more leaning heavily on the steering wheel, I hear God speak gently from within: "Forgive her."

In that moment, I know I have to either let God deal with my soul or not. I audibly speak the words, "Jesus, in your name, I forgive her. Her. I forgive her for causing my life to cease as I once knew it. I forgive her for having been so careless. I forgive her for making the terrible mistake that causes me such pain."

As the deep keening wail begins to be transformed supernaturally by the indwelling power of the Holy One, a penetrating stillness unlike anything I'd known before begins to cover me like a blanket.

I feel my face—soaked with tears. My body trembles, shakes, and spasms uncontrollably. I am aware that sweat has drenched every part of me; even my hair is dripping wet, again.

I feel my heavenly Father assure me. "Forgiveness is complete."

I feel a gentle prodding, a little nudge in my gut. "Oh no, Jesus," I cry, and tears burst forth again. "Please oh please let me stay here, Jesus."

I begin to hear the sounds of the vehicles on the road, and I begin to panic as I become aware of my surroundings. "Please, Jesus, let me stay. I can't live here if you go."

"O My child, My very own, I have put My words in your mouth and hidden you safely within My hand. You are Mine!" I actually hear these words.

Surprised, I reply, "But Lord Jesus, I can't remember anything or put words together so that they make sense. People look at me funny when I talk."

Immediately, I feel that now-familiar liquid warmth begin on my head and slowly flow over my entire body, all the way down to the ankles and toes. Supernaturally, I know He will put His words in my mouth when He wants them there.

My thoughts begin to be uncovered as I sit in my car. To really forgive this woman is the kindest thing I get to do for myself. It is the right thing … yes, the kindest thing. I set her free before my God while He's now unhooked me from unforgiveness. Grace and mercy set me free.

All I'm aware of in these moments is being in Jesus. He said it was so in John 15, and I hear Him remind me, "*Abide in Me, and I in you*" (John 15:4). I feel still and quiet, as though suspended in Him. It's a holy hush, and I'm inside that holy place where there's no room for doubt, fear, questions, answers, or any other form of dialogue. Only being. Being in Jesus. In that keeping, so completely unconditionally inside pure love. I long to be with Jesus like this forever. I am aching with painful longing to go "home." Heaven. Heaven is my home.

I'm held and loved in this place for a long time until I'm aware that I lack absolutely nothing. I barely breathe. This holy time of movement between my spirit and His indwelling Holy Spirit assures me that I am His, and that's all that matters. Everything here on earth pales and dims. I am at rest staying so still in His presence. This is no ordinary survival. I know. I'm present here, and I know with utmost assurance that Jesus is truly deeper than the deepest of the deep.

I acknowledge mercy while quietly sobbing. "Thank you! Oh, thank you! I don't have to stay here alone. You said you'd come here with me and you did. You're here. You're here!"

Joy begins like a bubble, but it pops as once again the heat of the intense July sun beats down upon my car. Joy perseveres and a determination mounts, even as the sensation of shaking and utter exhaustion filters through me. I know I asked Jesus to come with me back to this place where my life as I had known it up until one year ago came to a screeching halt. He is so present.

I lift my hand and feel the pain of my healing ribs, and silently I put my hand in His, only to be aware that I am already in Him with my heart. The physical lift of my hand is not needed. He has taken me through to this place of devastation and will lead me through the completion of rehabilitation and into a place of lifelong restoration.

God's assurance comes. "When you pass through the deepest waters, I am there."

Relief mingled with an audible sigh comes. Slowly I become more aware of the things of this world, but it's okay. It really is okay. He kept me then, keeps me now, and will continue to keep me. I'm sure not alone here on this earth where He left me.

The phrase Jesus spoke to my heart resurfaces, and I hear Him say, "There is a place deep inside called Courage."

"Yes," I acknowledge, "yes, there is. You, Jesus, are Courage."

A relief so profound settles into my inner being that all I can do is weep yet again until the deep pain of my soul enters the stillness of peace as He quiets me with His love.

Sitting in the car, I wonder. *What will I do? Who will I be?* I don't know. Christ in me, however, had already prepared that place so deep inside called Courage that at a time exactly like this, I'd be able to choose life. Abundant *life*! All the unnecessary intellectual processes within me were dead.

I sit in my burgundy Dodge Spirit in awe and wonder. It is exactly a year after everything in my mind and body broke during the crash. My spirit, though, is alive … more alive than ever before. Now in my car, God has me absolutely alone.

I smile for the first time. "He's rendered me utterly incapable of confounding logical intervention. He's imprinted himself into my being … I don't have a clue what that means, but that's okay."

I dry my tears, blow my nose, and start the car. I leave that place, that crash site, knowing that I left the awful power of dread behind.

The sheer joy of playfully rejoicing in grace comes when total surrender and forgiveness become complete. I know God is about to move me forward toward being restored. I hear the phrase Jesus spoke to my heart in that stinky old cab months before. It resurfaced. He reminded me: "There is a place deep inside called Courage."

"Yes," I acknowledge again, feeling fresh and clean. "Yes, there is! You, Jesus, are Courage."

I drive away toward my new life.

* * *

I had one more place to go after leaving the crash site on July 31, 2000. Full of courage and determination, I sped toward the RCMP station where I continued the business of my work to move forward and get well. For the first time in a year, songs of praises to God burst forth in my prayer language. I was driving after all, and needed to concentrate on the road in English (grin)!

Much like fresh mud being flung behind the wheels of a car, I headed away from Highway 8, down McPhillips Street, and sped toward Selkirk—the place that held one more piece of that accident day. My file was there. I needed to actually see the devastation Jesus had delivered me from. I had been told many details of the crash, but now I was ready to see pictures taken by the identification photographer. I pulled up beside the RCMP station, switched off the ignition, and stared at the station door. I didn't know what my body would do as I asked to see my file. Courage in the form of assurance came and I entered, leaning hard on my two canes. I shook from the day's exertion. I limped toward the dark-gray front counter across a rather gravelly, hard floor.

"May I help you?" asked a male officer, without looking up.

As bravely as possible, I stated, "My name is Hedy Wiebe, and I was in a severe motor vehicle accident on July 31, 1999." My heart pounded in my ears and I was conscious of the bile rising in my throat. "This is the f-f-file number my h-husband g-gave me," I stuttered, sliding the number across the counter. My head was doing the usual swimming and sloshing.

"You can't just see a file, madam," the officer countered abruptly. By now our eyes had met, and I was aware of three other officers who had stopped working. They were assessing the conversation at the front desk. All looked up and at me.

"I believe I can see this one, because I need to," I gulped, swallowing the rising bile.

A different officer stepped forward. "I'll take care of this. Come this way, Mrs. Wiebe. I'm the one your husband spoke to. A friend of mine called to make these arrangements for you."

He led me to a small room with yellow painted walls, and we sat on the only two chairs in the room. Probably an interrogation room—the only quiet, uninterrupted place in a police station. I sat down first. I heard the scraping metal of the chairs on the grey concrete floor.

"You're sure you want to do this?" asked the officer. I felt his eyes assessing me while he exercised his years of training to see if he was making a good judgement call. "Can you do this?" he asked again. His eyes looked like they could see straight inside me.

"I don't know," I whispered, "but I know I have to try."

I looked over at him, and out of my mouth I heard my voice say, "Jesus wants me well. I want to be well. I don't know what you guys saved me from. I need to see for myself. I need to feel gratitude so I can move on."

"You don't have to do this," he countered quietly. "I was there."

"You saw me?" I swallow hard as tears welled up in my eyes. "Thank you. I think I remember your eyes! You know you are looking at a miracle." I give him a lopsided kind of grin.

"Like I said, I was there. I'll get your file for you." He spoke softly, rising from his chair.

He came back and slid a closed folder in front of me. "Do you want me to stay?" he asked.

I looked at him as he waited, and I saw a man I didn't know yet felt I did. He'd helped pull me from that mangled heap.

"I'll need your purse," the officer stated, holding out his hand. "Do you have any other personal belongings on you?"

I'd been a police officer's wife for years and knew he was making sure that I didn't take pictures of the file or hurt myself with something while I was in there.

"Here's the number to call if I'm not okay," I tell him. "My girls made me take it, just in case. They know I'm here … I really need to do this alone with my Jesus. He'll help me."

A curt nod was his response as he closed the door behind him, leaving me to see, for myself, the incredible, utter devastation one person's careless mistake left behind.

I was alone. Alone in a room I knew had held many a person for questioning. Fleetingly, I think, *I didn't die so "she" wasn't charged.* Half-heartedly,

I hoped to read "her" name somewhere in the report; then I could say Carol or Janice or Marge—something other than "the mom of the four-year-old girl who didn't stop at a stop sign." She had made a terrible mistake. I was now about to look inside that manila file folder and see the aftermath of a car wreck.

I braced myself. A stiffness came over me; the inside of my head did its whirly-bird thing, my heart pounded, and my hands started to sweat. I felt the wave of trauma begin to build. I trembled.

"Not now, Jesus. Please not now." I pleaded with my ever-present God. "They'll come in and take me out and call the girls, and then I won't get to see. Please, Jesus."

Once again, the prayer language flowed naturally from my heart to my lips, and the softness of being filled by the Holy Spirit began. I felt Him physically calming all my body parts as the feelings of trauma slipped away.

"Thank you," I breathed in gratitude. "Yes, I know I'm not there now. Just keep me, my Lord."

It was time. I opened the folder and looked at the pages; I read about what I was saved from and how I got out of that car. I slid my finger to the top right of the folder and moved it down. Turning one page, I saw a typed report. Briefly flipping through the pages, I searched for pictures. Not a single one was in there! I read the prepared report, knowing it would have been pre-screened. Names, just like Don said, had been removed, except for the officer's signed reports.

Intermittently I needed to stop, close my eyes, and rest. The act of reading, having my eyes track from left to right, activated my nystagmus, and nausea and dizziness. I repeated the process of read/rest, read/rest. I didn't understand most of it, but I made myself read it all. I felt satisfied that what I'd been told was true. The accident was recorded as fact.

The truth that none of this was my fault made me decide that never again would I apologize for feeling like a burden, an inconvenience, or an intrusion. Nope, not to anyone, especially not an insurance company or someone assigned to help me.

I heard a gentle tap on the door as the officer asked, "Are you all right?"

I smiled, reassuring him as he entered this little room in which Jesus was healing me a bit more. I knew I looked determined.

"I'd like to see the photos now," I stated as I closed the folder.

"Pictures?" he repeated raising his eyebrows in concern. "I don't think that's a good idea, madam."

"Yes, it is," I stated slowly and clearly. "It is."

We looked at one another a long time. Through his eyes I could see the debate going on in his head.

I sighed and said, "After what I've lived through, I can do anything. They say I have organic amnesia. I don't have any recall. That's a blessing. No nightmares. But I need to see where I was. I want to see what you took me out of."

With a curt nod, he made his decision. This compassionate officer left and returned shortly with a tan envelope, which he handed to me.

"I'll be just outside," he said and left.

As I looked down at the second folder, I knew this was why I'd come. Jesus was about to do His thing, because I was most assuredly not alone. God's presence positioned me into a safety zone. I took a determined, deep breath, trusting Jesus to keep me no matter how my mind, body, and spirit responded. The assurance of His keeping was palpable. I knew I belonged to my beloved Lord and was covered with His banner of love. I knew that I knew that I knew. His tangible love had come. It blew out fear so that courage became real. Really real. Not ungraspable. I tasted something sweet in my mouth and instantly knew I had tasted and seen the goodness of God in that room.

I opened the envelope flap lying on that cold steel tabletop and slid my hand inside the opening. I could feel the glossy coating of a visual record with my fingertips. What lay inside depicted crunched, smashed metal that had left devastation in its wake. Therein lay the photos of destruction. I would see with my own eyes the beginning of where my life as I had known it stopped. I felt compelled to examine them and feel the loss. This hurt. Oh man! It hurt badly.

Unaware of my surroundings, time passed, and a supernatural calm that only exists in Jesus was the very air I breathed while looked at what was in my hand. I was alert in Jesus, completely abiding because He surrounded everything. I was in a holy place and on holy ground, because Jesus is God, and His Holy Spirit filled all of me. I could smell His fragrance again as I had before. I was ready.

Totally unafraid, I slid out the pictures and looked at the first one, the second, the third, and so on. I looked at the mashed wreck of a car. I had been in it and I survived! So had my dear friend.

Thoughts and feelings began to flip about inside me. There was no order or sequence. I was horrified! I was grateful. I see blue turquoise mangled metal that had been my friend's little cute Neon. The wheels were still on. As I continued through the pile of pictures, I saw more.

"That's where they must have used the jaws of life. The gouge on the grass was terribly deep! I was in that mess. That's where we hit the van."

My thoughts and verbal muttering continued. "There's burgundy paint on what once was a front end. The headlights are gone! How could we have fit in there? Amazing it didn't explode."

On and on came thoughts, crashing faster and faster until there were no more.

I asked Jesus, "Is there anything more I need to see? I don't want anything left undone. Nothing."

I spread the photos out like a fan before me and looked at them all again, waiting on Jesus to show me more. This time I saw the burgundy van on its side and the point of our impact just behind the mama driver's side. What a mangled mess!

"Oh Abba," I said, "I'm so glad that the little four-year-old lived and will have her mom. The little one has a mom!"

Tears slid down my cheeks, and I realized my Andrea and Aaron still had their mom too. Don still had his wife. I'd get to know Wilma … and maybe even grandkids!

"I'm alive!" I sobbed with joy. "I'll get to love them all!"

My deep sobbing produced concern on the other side of the closed steel door. I heard a light tap and then, "Are you okay?"

I felt a burst of gratitude rise in my gut and flow out of my lips as I answered the officer. "Yeah, I'm okay."

Staring teary-eyed at those pictures, I began to see not only the devastation but the depth of the place I'd been saved from. I both smiled and cried, "Lord Jesus, you saved my soul so long ago, and now you saved my body."

I don't have the ability to adequately describe what looking, seeing, touching, smelling, and feeling the photos of the car crash did for me and to me. It was like trying in vain to see enough and navigate through fog as thick as pea soup. Inside that Selkirk RCMP detachment room, I took my power back. I walked my way through the trauma. I was about to learn how to begin again. A new me. A better me. An unapologetic me. I owned every part of what had happened to me.

I physically raised my left hand, palm up, fully expecting the importation of the presence of the Holy Spirit to descend upon me. I mean really. Just as real as the pen in my hand and the photos on the cold table.

I closed my eyes, as the iridescent neon lights overhead hurt them. I waited, aware of the physical pain that had by now increased in my legs, hip, head, ribs, gut, and arm. Then slowly I felt the familiar presence of my Lord increase also. He came to me as I waited. I felt Him. My skin tingled and a slight shaking began, not to be confused with fatigue. My raised hand became increasingly warm, and the swirling feeling in my gut was not painful cramping. Then came peace.

Calm settled within my body like a liquid gold coating. The fog cleared from my mind. I could "see in the Spirit," and I knew I was being positioned to sit at the feet of Jesus. As I sat, I looked down at those photos. I utterly trusted the images into His keeping. He knew what I needed to see, and He would reveal what I needed to know. I opened my eyes and literally saw the wreckage from a supernatural vantage point.

I began to converse with Jesus with the easy, precious familiarity of safety. This way of becoming had become natural to me. Talking with God and He with me. I asked Him many questions in that room, much as a girl would ask her daddy.

"What's that? Where was I over there? Where was my sweet friend? How did I not get crushed? She says your peace filled in the car as it rolled. Thank you. Is that the window through which my glasses flew? That telephone pole is so close! I was told if we had rolled once more, we might not be alive! Is that true? The lady's van ... a darker maroon than I thought. Her child must have been terrified falling over and over inside that mess! We all flew and tumbled a long, long way from impact. Lord, I'm glad that woman in the van didn't roll into the oncoming traffic. She landed so close over there."

Slowly my questioning began to wind down, and the deep ache in my throat gave way to my familiar language of tongues. I knew I was asking, "What was happening to me while I was unconscious?"

He audibly answered me, "I held you."

My throat knotted and tears flowed as I basked in the descending *shekinah* glory of God's light. The entire room became bathed in His love and in the words of my heavenly Father. The warm, physical radiance of love, assurance, comfort, keeping, and courage covered and flowed throughout my body as I sat on that hard steel chair. He covered me once more with His liquid gold.

Trembling, I put my forehead down on my arms and rested. The work of stepping away from the impending fear of dread was over.

I knew it. I felt it.

God did what God does—watch over me, lead and guide, direct and grant me courage to choose. I chose. I made up my mind to choose to submit, surrender, relinquish, and accept. I was not going to become resigned to all the harm that had happened to me. The reasons and purposes in that past place became irrelevant. To dwell in the past would be dishonoring and offensive to my Jesus. I decided to give the Lord of my life permission to use it all—every awful second of the destructive devastation—any way He wanted. I really didn't care how He did it or if He did at all. That was His business.

A profound relief settled within the core of my soul, and a peacefulness infused what felt like every square inch of my body in that interrogation room. God spoke audibly once more: "This is who I am!"

Immediately, truth pierced me. "*I can do all things through Christ who strengthens me*" (Philippians 4:13, NKJV). I was free to be me. Simply me, and that was and still is a wonderful thing! What would that look like for me? I didn't care. Who would that be? I really didn't care. I only cared that I would be exactly who Jesus intended. That was all. Complete stillness filled the room, like a fog rolling over land.

I lifted my eyes toward Heaven and then down to flip through the photos. The mess was still before me on the glossy pages. A curious realization struck me as I spoke out loud. "I'm done. I'm done here."

Stacking the pictures, I slid them back into the manila envelope, noting the accident file number in black across the top. What for? Didn't matter. Wouldn't remember it anyway. I was done! Sure enough, there came the knock again and the officer's request to enter. I sighed and responded. "Yup. I'm done."

Rising and grinning from ear to ear, I handed the officer the file. His eyes reflected disbelief and suspicion as he looked at me. He did that quick surveillance glance around the room that police officers are trained to do. He scanned the room, as it were, for some evidence of the transformation he obviously saw in me. The perplexing look that crossed his face caused me to giggle. "God is a whole lot bigger than all this, and He sure is bigger than you or me."

"You all right?" he asked quizzically, probably wondering if he needed to make that backup phone call to a family member.

"Yup," I answered, still giggling and amazed at the joy beginning to rise. By now I was accustomed to the familiar physical feeling of something breaking inside of me when God did business with dread and fear! I knew this would be the last time I'd have to deal with that! I had room for "The More of God."

To the officer, however, I said, "Thanks. Thanks for making this available and for your kindness to me."

"You sure you're all right?" he asked again, discreetly looking at the purse he'd returned to me and my hands.

I almost laughed out loud. I could tell he was checking out whether I had taken "something" and was high. Poor guy ... he was only doing his job.

"You know something?" I told him, "Over twenty years ago, Jesus saved me from myself... as in saved my soul ... as in being born again. In there," I continued, pointing and tapping the files I'd handed over, "He saved me physically. Yeah, I'm okay. Actually, I'm really well. I've been given today. I don't know if I have tomorrow here on earth, but I do know I have today. If not here, then it'll be heaven." I grinned from ear to ear. "For me, sir, it's a win/win!"

He shook his head. I shook his hand. I knew my God would answer the many unasked questions of this man's heart. My part was done there.

On one hand I wondered if those in the office saw what I felt—the inexpressible, powerful presence of my God who had shown up and kept me. On the other hand, I didn't care. I was being carried out to my car by transforming power.

July 31, 2000 ended the fear of the dread. As I breathed deeply, I also knew I breathed in the beginning of a different recovery restoration … new courage. I felt like I could do anything going forward.

"See," God breathed into my body, "I make all things new."

"Yes, Lord, I know. I really, really do."

I started the engine of my Dodge Spirit in that Selkirk RCMP parking lot. Words to a song surfaced in my brain as I attempted to get enough air in my lungs to sing. All those months later, my voice still sounded different, but I knew it was a prayer of thanksgiving for all I had been given. I sang, making up new words to an old song by Christopher Beatty:

> This is holy ground,
> I'm riding on holy ground,
> For where you are my Lord
> There the ground is holy.
> I have holy hands,
> I'm driving with holy hands,
> For where you are
> There the ground is holy.

Smiling, I realized I had much to share with my family. I knew my girls, Andrea and Wilma, were anxiously waiting by the phone. Don knew I'd call him if I needed help, and Aaron would be somewhere trusting God to take care of me! I ask you … what's not to love about that?

I made the call and told the kids I was coming home … wrapped up and coming home.

* * *

I am being restored every day ... kind of like when you take an old junker of a car, replace parts, tinker and tweak and buff her down, and give that old girl new wheels and a fine new finish. That's me! Better than before. Different. Way more beautiful, because the presence of my heavenly Father holds me, keeps me, and invites me to visit that place deep inside He calls Courage again and again. That what my life's been like for over twenty years.

I've learned to sing again, and I give thanks by making up my own songs. "Full of hope, I'll come to you, Lord, and I'll go wherever you say— forever and until."

I put my hope in God to live in the moment, because I don't know if I'll have another. I hope I do, but I don't know. My life could be gone from earth in the next moment. But—not yet—and that is a good thing, a fabulously good thing!

The work of stepping away from the impending fear of the dread has been over for years. I left it behind that day, the dread of all the "what ifs" and "I may never ..." Gone. Done. This painful cleansing process was necessary. Letting God purify me and set me free required my personal response. Why would I not submit and surrender into this perfectly still, holy love of my Father?

A lot of stuff I thought was relevant to living a full life became irrelevant that day. Overthinking everything was thankfully one of those things. It's like the Holy Spirit blew His wind through my clogged-up brain and blew out the cobwebs that had been in stuck there. He was about to teach me that the best part of me was alive—alive to love, laugh, and live! Jesus indwells me through the power of the Holy Spirit. I was in awe that God had moved me to the keeping of grace, which is not irrelevant. Not at all.

I didn't wonder at the time about the fact that deep truly calls unto deep and He, the Keeper of the Deep, owns that place, because He bought and paid for it with the blood of His Son. Years later, I began to wonder and then understand what God did for me that day.

Later, when Jesus was alone with the twelve disciples and with the others who were gathered around, they asked him what the parables meant. He replied, "You are permitted to understand the secret of the Kingdom of God. But I use parables for everything I say to outsiders, so that Scriptures might be fulfilled."

—Mark 4:10–11

I too asked, "What did all that mean?" I wanted to know the secrets of God, but not from anywhere but the Bible. I read in Mark 4:12–13:

When they see what I do, they will learn nothing. When they hear what I say, they will not understand. Otherwise, they will turn to me and be forgiven … If you can't understand the meaning of this parable, how will you understand all the other parables?

My attitude became quite simple: "Please teach me, Lord. Please teach me to pray. Help me understand what I need to know to love you back." Over and over I've repeated these words. It takes courage to be brave and do what is right despite the fear of the unknowns.

God speaks all the time, and I sometimes get to hear Him when I'm listening. Jesus says, *"I am the good shepherd; I know my own sheep, and they know me"* (John 10:14). He goes on to say, *"My sheep listen to my voice: I know them, and they follow me"* (v. 27).

During those moments sitting in my car in the RCMP parking lot, I waited for my Lord to speak. I knew I'd hear Him talk to me, and I would let Him hold me just as I was, partially broken, partially mended, partially whole yet completely free to grow into who He said I already was. I was on a new journey to discover who this amazing woman I called "me" would become.

Chapter
eighteen

During the first several years after the accident, I'd sweated, grunted, cried, rejoiced, and focused my way through every inch of what homecare, home physiotherapy, vestibular therapy, Hedy therapy, family therapy, Don and me therapy, and PAR at HSC offered. I had learned to use a treadmill, the rowing bike, the thing that moves your ankles back and forth to build endurance, equipment for upper body strength, massages, stretches, exercises, and more. I could talk without stuttering all the time in a voice that sounded like my own. My eyes didn't want to close every waking moment. I had learned to balance myself so that I didn't drop things or fall as frequently. I started to use two canes more consistently for short distances. I even learned that the floor only *felt* like it moved as I walked.

A proud achievement occurred when I could dial a phone by myself without assistance. Numeric order is tough with some head injuries! I'd learned how to write my whole address from memory and no longer needed to copy it from a piece of paper. I'd also learned to drive around the block and find my way home!

There was much to relearn, but I had accomplished, with varying degrees of success, the tasks needed to become independent for short periods of time. My family became comfortable leaving me alone for longer periods.

Graduating out of PAR in June of 2000 deserved a happy dance! When asked where I would like to continue physiotherapy, I requested to be set up with Cindy Grant at River East Physiotherapy. This accomplished woman knew her stuff. Gullwing Transport would take me there in my wheelchair, because after physio, I was completely spent and needed to be taken home in that chair. Skillfully, she employed therapy that included acupuncture, water movement, manipulation, and endurance skills. Over the next several years, she helped me huff and puff my way into only needing that wheelchair for long distances, like when I went shopping. She taught me to fully use the two canes to my advantage until my balance improved enough that I only needed one.

During one particularly difficult session, I asked her, "Will I always be like this?"

Gotta love her answer. She replied, "Well, Hedy, not everybody gets to be hit by a Mack truck! You know what it feels like!"

Yessiree, I did!

Before the accident, I would not have counted small accomplishments as successes. I was an extrovert, used to being out front in most areas of my life, whether in front of the kids in my classroom, or in front of people as I sang. I talked a lot about a lot. The accident changed me. For the first time ever, I began to know what an introvert felt like. I was happy to be left alone. I longingly looked for a door whenever I was out somewhere as soon as the room closed in on me. Many unfamiliar feelings and reactions.

For travelling longer distances, I still needed my wheelchair. That thing was one trustworthy little roller. Yippee!

My first independent trip included a ride in the transport van to the most exciting event *ever* … a shopping trip to a mall where *all* the floors had smooth tile! My other wheelchair-bound friend and I had great fun that day!

* * *

As I worked with vestibular physio at HSC Rehab and Cindy, I gained physical strength as my body healed. God has a cool way of putting things back together. I call it "living in continuous healing." But physical balance continued to be a real issue. No matter how hard I worked, I still tipped and stumbled to the right every time I moved my head or body the "wrong" way. I'd learned to straddle my legs, which now held me up as the canes added to my stability, but the vertigo continued. What a stinker! Nasty business, that! That short-circuited and prevented me from progressing, much to the dismay of insurance companies. I think they like to wrap up a file in about five years. Ah, I wanted out too! But I knew this was not my fault. I was a passenger; I didn't have to prove I'd been hit in that accident, and I was determined to get well-er and well-er!

Long before July 31,1999, the words written by King David in Psalm 27 had enlarged my heart so that God's peace in the presence of anything prevailed. Years before, God, through the death of His Son, Jesus, and upon the impartation of His truth through His Holy Spirit, had blessed me with the knowledge of His faithfulness to me no matter what. He is who He says.

Because God is, I would have despaired had I not believed I would see *"the goodness of the Lord in the land of the living"* (Psalm 27:13b, NIV). The King James version says, *"I had fainted, unless I had believed to see the goodness of the Lord in the land of the living."* In the NLT, the verse reads, *"Yet I am confident I will see the Lord's goodness while I am here in the land of the living."* That was me. It was how I felt assured again and again as I put myself through the paces of becoming who I was now meant to be. Those words helped me.

The word *goodness*, however, took a totally different turn. Before the accident, I understood goodness in earthly terms of what I could do or what was done to or for me. It didn't matter one whit that I couldn't and didn't have "brain nor brawn," as the saying goes. All I knew for sure was that Jesus was holding me, orchestrating all matter of things around me, in me, and through me. I sure didn't have to have my words "right," especially when I talked with my Lord. Grateful for the gift of tongues? Yeppers!

The "stick to it like stink" thinking that accompanies rehabilitation progression wasn't always a walk in the park. Some days just stank! However, I had those who encouraged and prayed for me.

Around February 2001, after my time at River East Physiotherapy, I was sent to The Wellness Centre at the Seven Oaks Hospital, where the first ambulance had arrived with me after the crash. Full circle. But now I was in a waaaaaay different department, far away from the ER.

I thought I'd arrived. What a fabulous facility! It had everything under one roof. I learned to use gym equipment tailored to my needs. A steam room relaxed my muscles after working hard, and I saw myself improve. It was there that I started to feel physically strong.

I still often had vestibular episodes. Years later they called them BPPV—Benign Paroxysmal Positional Vertigo. When I had an episode, I looked like I was having a seizure. The nystagmus would set in, my eyes rolled back, my head movements looked weird, my speech slurred, and my body stopped functioning as I slumped. I had learned what to do: pray and hang on and try not to pass out!

Others knew who to call: Don. I did not want to go to the hospital. I wanted my bed or to my vestibular therapist, who would perform an "Epley manoeuvre," which was an attempt to get crystals in the inner ear back to where they belonged! Years later, I learned how to do this myself or with my family's help without passing out. I absolutely detest when that occasionally still happens.

Chapter
nineteen

GOD HAS DESIGNED A PURPOSE AND A PLAN FOR MY LIFE. IT'S A PLAN that only I can fulfill. It doesn't require the actions of anyone else, but it does rely heavily on my willingness to go where I'm called by the Lord and then do what I am to do. I must, however, be willing to seek what God has for me. This requires that I regularly surrender to Him, trusting that He has a plan.

Accidents happen all the time. People get well from head injuries and broken messes. Many heal from broken bodies, but some not so much or at all. Ever. I don't get to have answers for everything. There are always scars where hurt began, both inside and out. But I believe with all my heart that mine don't have to define me. I use them to know more of the nearness of God.

During times of great struggle, healing work took place that I didn't even know about, but I believed that Jesus's pain on my behalf had a purpose. I'd witnessed enough supernatural miracles in and around me to know that Jesus alone is enough. He is the Son of God. He is the greatest miracle, and He has already enabled me to believe that out of His pain, I was saved. What a miracle that is! His courage to die for me has given me a purpose to live. That horrible accident got turned around, and God used the awful times to call me into closer relationship with Himself. It changed me. The Bible tells us that miracles glorify God.

At times in the ups and downs, or ebb and flow of my life, both before the accident and after, I've wearied of being changed. I've yelled, "Enough! Stick a fork in me; I'm done!" I've wasted my energy on "I can't," "I don't want to," or, "It's none of my business" stuff. I'm not afraid to fall or step into Jesus just as I am, without needing to clean myself up first. What a relief! He is the restorer, not me.

More often, though, I've given myself permission to not fritter away the moments, days, or years given to me as a gift. I decide or choose what I focus on. I love feeling invigorated and being curious to seek out what God may have "just around the next corner!" If I choose wisely, I can be assured that the wind of His Holy Spirit will blow on my teeny, or barely flickering, flame of light. His powerful love will ignite my soul with His consuming fire (Luke 12:49). I long for every heart to be ablaze with the fire of God!

I love being lit up by God, but I don't always like the process. It hurts to have my heart broken, but to have it broken for the things that break the heart of my friend Jesus hurts way more. No, I don't like my heart broken, but I know that where it breaks, I'll have more room for His love to flow. I'll be more useful in some way. Nothing is ever wasted, because I am in His will.

During each process, whether the destruction of being in the way of a careless mistake, or the grunt work of sweating my way back to living on my feet, God has never left me broken and alone. He promised me He wouldn't, and He never breaks a promise. Ever. People have told me that they think I survived the car crash because God needs me here on earth. To that I say, "Pish posh!" I have need of *Him* here.

My Abba God kept me in the broken places. It was out of Him that the place deep inside called Courage was birthed in me and found a purpose. It was critical care for me. I needed to know Him there to survive. I had learned that it's simply profound and profoundly simple: reflect Jesus here on earth. His death on the cross had already made that possible. The Bible tells me "… *the Lord has told you* (Hedy) *what is good, and this is what He requires: to do what is right, to love mercy, and to walk humbly with your God*" (Micah 6:8).

The accident that screeched my life to a halt for a while propelled me into something different. If it had not happened, I would have learned what God wants me to know of Him in another way. It was like I had been thrown into a crucible where I not only survived but came out changed.

The Bible teaches that a crucible is used for making silver and gold into something with great value and purpose. The metals become crazy hot and then the silversmith or goldsmith fashions it according to his will. It turns out so shiny after it's been hammered and polished, it can be made into anything—something beautiful. I was in that refining pot a long time. I am beautiful to my Lord. Proverbs 27:21 says, "The crucible is for silver and the furnace for gold, and each is tested by the praise accorded him" (NASB).

I've come out of this crucible as a woman whose heart is strong, refined, and molded, totally unafraid of being tested again, because I trust my heavenly Father to know how to do that for good. He is, after all, good all the time. I'm glad I understand the word "good" differently now.

I have been formed into someone whose purpose, for a while, was solely about the business of getting well. During those years, I was repeatedly blessed to have Christ-followers pray for me, because they had been filled with power given from our Most High God. Healing through Jesus has already come. He's already done it all, don't ya know it?

In Romans 8:26–28, Paul says:

And the Holy Spirit helps us in our weakness. For example, we don't know what God wants us to pray for. But the Holy Spirit prays for us with groanings that cannot be expressed in words. And the Father who knows all hearts knows what the Spirit is saying, for the Spirit pleads for us believers in harmony with God's own will. And we know that God causes everything to work together for the good of those who love God and are called according to his purpose for them.

I mean, how great is *that*? He used the whole mess that was not meant for good and made me into the woman I am today. He made me into a "good thing." Christ knew that to endure the pain, I had to be in His keeping. He had a purpose in mind.

My personal life continues because I have moved through the devastation, worked hard during the rehabilitation (and still need to at times), and now live in places of joyful restoration created by God—one day at a time! Each day is a gift in which to be me.

Joyful restoration is the process and choice of being. It's not an event. It's a lifelong journey here on this earth. God infuses *joy* again and again, right alongside incredible pain, sorrow, grief, repentance, disappointment, celebration, and surrender. The great final event will be when I get to step into Heaven and stay!

"It is in the quiet crucible of your personal private sufferings that your noblest dreams are born, and God's greatest gifts are given in compensation for what you've been through. It is well."[1]

---

1   "Wintley Phipps Quotes," AZ Quotes, accessed February 26, 2020, azquotes.com/quote/767726

Reflections

New beginnings are sometimes blurry. I can't pinpoint when a change began to occur. It unfolded slowly and it's placement in the timeline remains elusive. The restorative processes were like that. My physical body was healing, but as soon as I was vertical for more than twenty minutes, both ankles ached. Right shoulder muscular pain presented with movements like reaching, lifting, or lying down on it. Thankfully, after a year, the ribs had healed well, my back was no longer black and blue, and I could once again take deeper breaths.

I cried the day I tried to sing like I had before, when most notes were within easy reach. I was incredibly disappointed by the sounds my vocal cords produced. Since then, God has healed me, so I'm able to sing again … not like before, but worshipping God with what I have now brings me joy and happiness. I sing more in my prayer language, and the desire to show the Lord how much I love and adore Him by using this gift has often lifted physical pain, sorrow, and disappointments. It has filled me with supernatural rest and lasting peace. I can't adequately express how grateful I am that the Comforter, my Keeper, comes and touches me over and over with His blessings.

On this earth in our human bodies we'll experience good days and not so good days. I don't know what it's like not to have both hips hurt. I'm grateful for the occupational therapist who insisted the insurance company pay for a RoHo butt cushion. I used to take it with me everywhere for comfort. Today it's in my car because it helps absorb the jarring of the road up the spine, neck, and into my ears while in a vehicle.

For the first five or six years after the accident, I don't remember not having gut issues that made me feel like I had a gastrointestinal infection. The worst part, however, was living with the continuous nausea and dizziness from morning 'till night. One morning I woke up cross. I recall being ticked off. Spitting mad, as a matter of fact! Not the best day, but a real one. The unedited version of what I wrote started with …

Living with the Nausea

Here it is five years later, and my head's still spinning, my eyes still hurt, and flickering light drives me nuts! My gut still feels like I'm going to throw up, but I never do! I wish that I could barf and make it finally go away. I've had it with being sick to my stomach! Quite frankly, Jesus, I'm so sick of being nauseous, I could puke! As if that would help. Stupid head! Stupid vertigo! Stupid everything! Crappy day!

Once again, I've got to make this pathetic, desperate call. The call will begin a cycle of vestibular physio at HSC and acupuncture with a therapist … again. Grrr. That means leaving what I want to do and getting someone to drive me yet again. I've got to get stabilized so I can drive alone. I hate starting all over. If running away from myself worked, I would. My self just follows me wherever I go, like an irritating Manitoba Mozzie (one of our large mosquitoes). Somebody please smack it or help me smack it. If I wasn't so darned dizzy, I'd find the "spot" of trouble myself and smack it! What nonsense! I'm talking utter nonsense, but that's how I feel—sick of being sick!

* * *

Looking back over those years, I'm grateful I had medical people who helped me get well. I've had years of intermittent medication, physiotherapy, and acupuncture for physical strengthening or maintenance. Twenty years later, I call myself a "frequent flyer," accessing help when needed. Everybody's brain is a muscle with the capacity for memory. Lots are good and helpful for me, but sometimes the memories aren't so good. About five months after the accident, the not-so-good surfaced, and I began to work with Dr. Ian Mogilevsky, a Christian clinical psychologist. This fine man helped me sort and slot what had happened in my brain and my body, and what was unfolding in my soul. I think this was when the first inklings of a restorative process began in my mind through thoughtful surrender and learning to trust God with what my different life might become.

Over these many years, I've learned to wade through the waters, away from the devastation, through the various rehabilitation stages, and into places of restoration. At times I've felt a bit like Pinocchio when he became a real boy. He realized he was truly alive. I know that feeling. He danced, sang, and happily rejoiced. I did and do too! Repeatedly!

I've learned what it means to live in my Father's place of restoration and that it's not a one-time event, even though I wanted it to be. I wanted to be done with it and restored like the guy who buys an old beater of a car, and then turns it into a shiny, originally restored 1957 Chevy. Sigh. Not how it works.

As time passed, I became more aware that I had been blessed by God with the determination to move through the events that had or were occurring and to use those times as stepping stones to make me better, not bitter. God showed me what His divine love feels and looks like. It meant learning to extend grace to others. I had already been given His amount, which is enough in every situation.

As the journey of restoration continues today, I no longer resent my weaknesses. His love for me enters my weakness and provides what He knows I need. I figure that's a pretty good deal! I agree with Him and He fills me. Jesus shows up, especially when I believe the time is 11:59.

"And He said to me, 'My grace is sufficient for you, for My strength is made perfect in weakness'" (2 Corinthians 12:9a, NKJV). The overflow of this truth helped during the first and second year after the collision, when it was hard to keep my head steady. My eyelids often felt heavy and drooped shut. At times it was impossible to keep them open. Overwhelming fatigue seeped into and throughout my body. Sometimes I knew an angel's presence. I didn't see one physically all the time, but I knew without a doubt that God had sent one. I recall specific times when I physically saw the angel with my eyes wide open. He was huge, and it was always the same one. I know I was given insight to know this one was male and sent to watch over me.

In Colossians, the apostle Paul teaches us that angels are God's messengers. They are spiritual beings created by God and totally under His authority. One of an angel's functions is to serve God in any way He instructs (Hebrews 1). Another way is to protect the helpless (Matthew 18). Well, I was helpless, and I was being served, both by humans and angels. Both were as plain as the nose on my face.

I don't have the English words to describe the two angels leaning in the back of the ambulance, or the one standing in the doorway when Don was furious at the hospital. Nothing comes close to describing what I felt lying in the hospital bed when a warm touch brushed across my cheek, and I'd open my eyes to see who had come in, but no human was there. Then there was the day I clearly saw the angel. He stood ramrod straight like a sentinel guard the day the crazy homecare lady came to the house. He was also the one assuring me the day I felt at my loneliest moment.

* * *

Around five months into recovery, I had a new beginning, but it wasn't a "purrr-dy one," as they say. It happened shortly after the third traumatic episode in which I thought I'd die in that "tsunami wave." It was the darkest time in my recovery. Silently and secretly, I had convinced myself that I was a burden to everyone, and I was mad that I'd been left on this earth. I felt unloved by God.

One morning when I was feeling especially low, I switched on the TV. Guess what was on? Yup! *100 Huntley Street* with David Mainse. For a moment I debated shutting it off so I could stay in my misery. "Jesus," I shouted. "This is *not* funny!"

I continued to watch, but I was mad. "I don't want to be here!" I said to God. "I want to come Home! I want to quit! I've made life miserable for Don and the kids. I won't stay on this earth without the tangible evidence of your love for me." My sobbing was more like a pathetic, sick lion roar.

"Okay, okay … I'll call in." I grumbled. Dialing a phone successfully was still a sequencing issue for my brain. A bunch of tries to get the numbers right and I heard a ringing. The person answering got the full weight of my grief. Silence.

A woman on the line spoke lovingly. "Hedy, I recognize your voice. It's me, Ruth."

"Who?" I asked, confused. I knew several women named Ruth.

"We saw the flower gardens in Niagara-on-the-Lake several years ago. We used to pray together. I heard what happened to you."

The 1-800 number I'd dialled went to centres all across Canada, but God had switched stuff around so that she'd get my call.

She went straight into the throne room of God with my pleading request to not stay on earth without the tangible evidence of His love for me. Immediately, my sobbing stopped, my hand raised in praise, and I felt His love descend with warm liquid gold flowing over me. I knew I was, am, and that I'd always be loved by Him.

Then my Rescuer spoke audibly to my heart: "My love is constant for you. Believe in Me."

This godly friend told me she had a verse she'd like to read to me. She also said I would come to know the meaning of each word well. I can't count how many times I've read the following verse:

> The Lord will comfort Israel (Hedy) again and have pity on her ruins. Her desert will blossom like Eden, her barren wilderness like the garden of the Lord. Joy and gladness will be found there. Songs of thanksgiving will fill the air.
>
> —Isaiah 51:3

I had been revived and once more knew that I was not a burden. I was a gift. The darkness left.

* * *

I remember back to the first few days at home from the hospital. I wasn't aware of much. I was coughing. It was painful, and Don had been downstairs praying for my chest to heal. I felt a warm hand on me. I thought it was my husband, but he hadn't come upstairs. One more time I saw the same angel standing guard by my bedroom door, bringing comfort and rest because the pain was more than I could stand.

Many times I'd know to look to my right and lift my eyes, sensing someone was there. One day, a visiting friend remarked as she looked around our bedroom in wonder, "There are angels in here!" She saw them that day. I did not.

I could only smile and reply, "Yes, I know."

My friend and I worshipped God together and gave thanks for His kindness, in humble adoration of the one who is Comfort.

Gratitude is a word that describes how I feel looking back and remembering. I'm grateful the Bible is full of accounts of people meeting angels. Angels worship and serve God all the time. That's their function. I believe God when He says He has given His angels charge over me and that they bear me up in their hands (Psalm 91). We aren't to worship angels or think that they're at our beck and call. When something amazing happens, we shouldn't credit them for it. Often we refer to kind people as "angels." Sometimes when someone special dies, people take comfort in the thought that she/he is now an angel in heaven, but it's just not biblically true. God tells us in His word that He has already created all the angels, and they are His.

Those who have seen or experienced the presence of a true angel of light know that the ministering spirit was sent by Almighty God. That person will never be casual or flippant about it again. I know I won't be. I won't even wonder if that angel was real. I just know.

I'm fascinated by how God has used angels through the ages and throughout His Word, a love letter to us all. I'm thankful for each moment my eyes saw a glimpse of Jesus and His angels. Someday, in heaven … well, for now I'm limited in my imaginings and wonder, for I live here on this earth.

* * *

In 2000, I felt like a butterfly emerging from its cocoon as spring came to our Winnipeg, Manitoba yard. I had a revived sense of appreciation for the newness of normal life as it continued all around me. The smell of freshly cut grass filled my senses as though I were smelling it for the first time. I remembered daisies were my favourite flower. The petals seemed whiter as they sassily swayed in the warm breeze.

One day that spring a wonderful friend showed up at our door. Without a word, she set up the wheelchair ramps at the front door, wrapped me in a blanket, plopped me into the wheelchair, and whipped me down those ramps into the sunshine. She'd brought me a yogurt smoothie, which we enjoyed outside. She took my hand and said, "You've worked hard enough for now, I think. It's time to celebrate!" We laughed and drank our smoothies. That was the day I began to experience many new beginnings, and they weren't blurry at all. From then on, I intentionally began to celebrate moments, then days, then the life I still had to live. That afternoon, I hauled out an old binder, found a pen, crawled into bed, and began to scribble-scrawl words rambling around in my thoughts. Since then, over the many years, countless words, phrases, prayers, and short stories have tumbled onto paper. A few meander through the pages in this book. But that day I wrote the following poem. Each time I read it, I remember why my heart rejoices as I celebrate life here on this earth, where I get to love and be loved.

Celebrate

Celebrate Life
Just as it is!
Celebrate Life
Much is amiss!
Celebrate Life
Let Christ reign;
Celebrate Life
He keeps me sane.
Celebrate Life
Do I hear His Voice?
Celebrate life
Yes! I have made my choice.
Celebrate life!
Banishing angry rights.
Celebrate Life
Use His sword for fights.
Celebrate Life!

Guaranteed joy is mine.
Celebrate Life!
Jesus, you're divine.
Yes, I'll
Celebrate Life!

www.ingramcontent.com/pod-product-compliance
Lightning Source LLC
LaVergne TN
LVHW051559080426
835510LV00020B/3050